Fat Girls
and
Lawn Chairs

Fat Girls and Lawn Chairs

CHERYL PECK

WARNER BOOKS

NEW YORK   BOSTON

Copyright © 2002, 2004 by Cheryl Peck
All rights reserved.

This book was previously self-published by the author.

Warner Books

Time Warner Book Group
1271 Avenue of the Americas, New York, NY 10020
Visit our Web site at www.twbookmark.com.

Printed in the United States of America

First Printing: January 2004
10 9 8 7 6 5 4 3 2

Library of Congress Control Number: 2003048578
ISBN: 0-446-69229-8

Cover design by Brigid Pearson
Cover photo by Meredith Parmelee/Getty Images

Dedicated to D. Eloise Molby Peck, 1927–1976

acknowledgments

I would like to thank Trudi and Elin who spent years musing aloud, "Why don't you just write down the stories you tell?" until I finally did; *Lavender Morning* for allowing me to see my work in print; the Phoenix Community Church for sitting still for sometimes an hour at a time while I read to them; Annie for tirelessly reading everything I have handed her over the years; and my family for their sense of humor, which is nearly as twisted as mine.

I would like to thank Ranee Bryce, Teresa Terrill, Mary Jaglowski, Janean Danca and Pam Wong-Peck for proofreading this manuscript and discovering all of those errors that fell below my radar. I would particularly like to thank Ranee for doing it all over again five months later.

I would also like to thank Mary Appelhof, an internationally known author, for her publishing expertise and support. Historically she has been unfailingly supportive of aspiring authors and she is a strong voice in the publishing and environmental communities.

I would like to thank our mayor, Tom Lowry, whose wonderful bookstore was the first home for *Fat Girls*, and whose support of our efforts helped lead us to a contract with the Warner Book Group.

I would like to thank Amy Einhorn—my editor in New York—for her patience, her faith in me, and for allowing me to actually say to people I've known all of my life, "Amy—my editor in New York—says . . ."

None of you would be reading this without the tireless patience, confidence, support—and skills—of my Beloved, Nancy Essex. She hates attention and she is driven to make worthwhile all of our time spent here on earth—the two traits every undisciplined writer needs in a partner. I wrote it: everything beyond that point is her work and determination, not mine, and I thank her.

contents

introduction

JEFF DANIELS doesn't know me. He could if he wanted to: we ate in the same restaurant at the same time once. He was busy talking to the bartender and never once looked my way, but if he had he could have walked over and introduced himself and we could have become friends. I feel I have a special interest in Jeff and his career because, like me, he lives in a small town in Michigan just off interstate I-94. My truck, Hopalong, broke down in his hometown once. I used to work with a man whose kids went to school with his. Our lives intersect and overlap on a regular basis.

When you live in the Midwest like I do, celebrities are a rarity. I used to know a woman who lived just down the road from Ted Nugent, but I was always afraid that if I wandered too close to his property he would kill me and grill me. I've never felt that sense of kindredness and likeness of character with Ted that I feel with Jeff. While I am a fair hand at the air guitar, I'm afraid I would have to say that for a Midwesterner, Ted is a little out there. Jeff and I could find common ground.

I have always felt Jeff and I would get along well because, like me, he is a writer. At the age of thirteen I began writing the great American novel on a $10 typewriter I bought from an office supply store. I set my sights midway between James Joyce and T. S. Eliot (neither of whom I had read, I suspect, at thirteen) and I wrote passionately, dramatically and with great meaning for the next thirty-odd years. I never finished anything except the occasional Oscar acceptance speech. (Imagination is a vital ingredient to any writing career.)

During those thirty years my friends would listen to me rant on about my inability to produce great literature. They would say, "Why don't you just write down the stories you tell us?"

But those stories were about my cats, my family and the misadventures of a woman of size. They were not the stuff of great literature. And I did not "write" those stories; they were just spontaneous verbal riffs.

Some of my friends, in the meantime, published a small newsletter for the lesbian community in Kalamazoo, Michigan, and they were always begging for articles. Finally—after much persuasion—I tentatively wrote a short, humorous article about cat hair. I followed that with an article about the birth of my (then) youngest niece. My reading audience swelled to five or six. Soon I was encouraged to read my writings aloud at a talent show put on by the community church, where my audience burgeoned into the teens. My cat, Babycakes, became a literary character.

None of my siblings remember our history the same way I do. Some claim I spent most of our childhood wandering around in the gravel pit behind our property where I talked mostly to imaginary friends, as if the historical accuracy of a lunatic were automatically suspect. They have pointed out small inaccuracies in every story. My response to all of this is as follows: I write fiction.

I do have two younger sisters and two younger brothers. In the stories I have identified us in degrees of wee-ness: I am the Least Wee, my next younger sister is the UnWee (my favorite title—it sounds like "ennui" and reflects her innately less excitable nature), our baby sister is the Wee One (and when, at forty-one, she finally had her daughter, I dubbed the baby the Weeest). We three girls were born within a five-year span; our Little Brother (1) is nine years younger than I am and our Baby Brother (2) is twelve years younger than I am. He attended kindergarten the same year I graduated from high school. We don't use such formal titles among ourselves. We just call each other by name. My age, my father's age, and the exact number of offspring of the reproductive among us changes from one story to the next because over time these things do. I did hit the Wee One in the head with a rock. She lived anyway. Her version of the story is different from mine, but hers is remarkably good-natured.

I grew up in rural Branch County, four miles north of Coldwater, Michigan. Our house is roughly twenty-five miles from the Michigan-Indiana state line. We lived in an old farmhouse, but by the time we moved there most of the farm had been turned into a gravel pit and our yard was cradled on two sides by a kidney-shaped 120-acre hole in the ground. Like much of southern Michigan, the area where I grew up is farm country dotted with small wooded areas, wetlands and lakes. It is pretty country without calling undue attention to itself. Legend has it that no one who lives in Michigan lives more than five miles from a lake—we lived across the road and a cornfield from a chain of five of them. When I was growing up small farmers believed their way of life was the safest, most reliable way to make a living and always would be. People were connected to the land. People did not just recklessly move around from here to there, and change was greeted with a skeptical eye.

I have not lived an extraordinary life and I did not have an unusual childhood. (I have long felt crippled by this as a writer.) I have tried to write honestly about the things I know about— what it's like to sit in a fishing boat with your father for an entire

Sunday morning when you are four years old and the longest time you've ever spent doing one thing is seven minutes . . . dealing with the dog your loving parents don't realize hates you when you and he are about the same size . . . why fat girls are wary of lawn chairs.

I am an oldest child. We oldest children like to keep everyone happy, smiling and in a good mood. We try not to hurt anyone's feelings. We have all of the characteristics of a good baby-sitter, which when you think about it, makes perfect sense. So welcome to my book. Sit down, make yourself comfortable. Have a good time. I'm expecting Jeff to call me anytime now, but until then, I'm all yours.

queen of the gym

It HAPPENED AGAIN this morning. I was sitting there half-naked on a bench when a fellow exerciser leaned over and said, "I just wanted to tell you—I admire you for coming here every day. You give me inspiration to keep coming myself."

"Here" is the gym.

I have become an inspirational goddess.

In a gym.

I grinned at the very image of it, myself: here is this woman who probably imagines herself to be overweight—or perhaps she is overweight, she is just not in my weight division—sitting on the edge of her bed in the morning, thinking to herself, "There is that woman at the gym who is twenty years older than I am and has three extra people tucked under her skin, and she manages to drag herself to the gym every day . . ."

It is not my goal here to be unkind to myself or to others. Perhaps I am an inspiration to her because I am easily three times her size and I take my clothes off in front of other women. Being fat and naked in front of other women is an act of courage. Perhaps my admirer did not realize that it was exactly when she spoke to me that I was artfully arranging my hairbrush and underwear and bodily potions to cut the buck-naked, ass-exposing mini-towel-hugging moments of my gym experience to the absolute minimum. She wears a pretty little lace-edged towel-thing to the shower and back. I don't, but I understand the desire.

It was not that long ago that she bent over to pick up something as Miss Tri Athlete walked into the locker room and whistled, "Boy did I get a moon!" Junior high gym, revisited: I can't swear that particular exchange was the reason, but I did not see my admirer again for the next month. To Miss Tri Athlete she answered, "Just when I had forgotten for half a second that I was totally naked . . ." I doubt that she forgets that often. Almost none of us do.

Nor do I: which is why, the first time someone in the locker room said to me, "I have to give you credit just for coming here," I smiled politely and thought ugly thoughts for some time afterwards. *Up yours* thrummed through my mind. *Nobody asked you for credit* zinged along on its tail, followed closely by *Who died and left you queen of the gym?*

"Like it takes any more for me to go the gym than it does any other woman there," I seethed to my Beloved.

"Well it does," my Beloved returned sedately, "and you know it. How many other women our size have you seen at our gym?"

The answer is—none.

There are women of all shapes and sizes—up to a point—from Miss Tri Athlete, who runs in the 20–25-year-old pack, wears Victoria's Secret underthings and is self-effacing about her own physical prowess to women who are probably in their sixties, perhaps even seventies. There are chubby women and postpartum moms and stocky women and lumpy women . . . but there are very few truly fat women.

Exercise, you might advise me solemnly, is hard for fat women.
Exercise is hard for everyone.
Exercise is as hard as you make it.

fat girls and lawn chairs

Miss Tri Athlete shared a conversation with me the other morning. She said, "It feels really good to get this out of the way first thing in the morning, doesn't it? I think when you plan to exercise in the evening it just hangs over you like a bad cloud all day." She can't be more than twenty-five, she can't be carrying more than six ounces of unnecessary body fat and I've never seen her move like anything hurts. Her joints don't creak. Her back doesn't ache. She sweats and turns pink just like everybody else. She trains like an iron woman, but she's relieved when it's over.

I don't believe it's exercise that keeps fat women out of the gym. I think it's the distance from the bench in front of the locker to the shower and back. I think it's years and years of standing in grocery lines and idly staring at the anorexic women on the cover of *Cosmo*, I think it's four-year-olds in restaurants who stage-whisper, "Mommy—look at that FAT lady," I think it's years of watching American films where famous actresses never have pimples on their butts or stretch marks where they had kids. It's *Baywatch*. Barbie. It's never really understanding, in our gut, that if we could ask her even Barbie could tell us exactly what is wrong with her body. And we all know, intellectually, of course, that Barbie's legs are too long, her waist is too short, her boobs are too big and her feet are ridiculous, but she's a doll. What we do not know, as women, is that my sports physiologist, who is in her late twenties and runs marathons, also has tendonitis in her shoulder, a bad back, and passes out if she trains too hard. My former coach for the Nautilus machines had MS. None of us have perfect bodies. If we did have perfect bodies, we would still believe we are too short or too fat or too skinny or not tan enough.

None of us have ever been taught to admire the bodies we have.

And nothing reminds us of our personal imperfections like taking off our clothes. Imagining that—for whatever reason—other people are looking at us.

My sports physiologist is more afraid of wounding me than I am of being wounded. The program she has set up for me to regain my youthful vim and vigor is appropriately hard. Not too hard, not too easy. It's just exercise. The most difficult part of my routine, designed by my physiologist, is walking through the heavy-duty weight room to get the equipment I need for my situps. The weight room is full mostly of men. Lifting weights. Not one of them has ever been rude to me, not one of them has even given me an unkind glance: still, the irony that I make the greatest emotional sacrifice to do the exercise I like the least is born again each time I walk into the room.

Someone might laugh at me.

Someone might say, "What are you doing here?"

I have a perfectly acceptable answer.

I joined the gym because my girlfriend said, "I want to walk the Appalachian Trail." I have no desire to backpack across the wilderness: but I could barely keep up with her when she made this pronouncement, and I could see myself falling farther and farther behind if I stayed home while she trained. I joined the gym because I used to work out and I used to feel better. Moved better. Could tie my shoes. I joined the gym because I dropped a piece of paper on the floor of my friend's car and I could not reach down and pick it up. I joined the gym because I have a sedentary job and a number of aches and pains and chronic miseries that are the result of being over fifty and having a sedentary job. I joined the gym because my sister, who is younger than I am and more fit, seriously hurt her back picking up a case of pop. It could have been me. It probably should have been me.

I keep going back to the gym because I love endorphins. I love feeling stronger. More agile. I can tie my shoes without holding my breath. I can pick papers up off the car floor without having to wait until I get out of the car. I don't breathe quite as loudly. I have lost that doddering, uncertain old lady's walk that made strange teenaged boys try to hold doors or carry things for me.

I keep going back because I hate feeling helpless.

Years ago, a friend of mine convinced me to join Vic Tanney, a chain of gyms popular at the time. There was a brand-new gym just around the corner from where we lived—just a matter of a few blocks. She had belonged to Vic Tanney before, so she guided me through the guided tour, offering me bits of advice and expertise along the way . . . I plopped down money, she plopped down money, and a few days later it was time for us to go to the gym.

She couldn't go.

She was fat.

Losing weight had been her expressed goal when she joined: now she couldn't go until she was "thinner."

Everyone else at the gym, she said, was buff and golden.

"I'll be there," I pointed out (for I have never been a small woman).

She couldn't go. She was too fat.

She was a size twelve.

I have determined that I don't particularly mind being the queen of my gym. There may indeed be women who wake up in the morning and sit on the edges of their beds and think to themselves, "There is that fat woman at my gym who goes almost every day, and if she can do it . . ." I am proud to be an inspirational goddess. It has taken me most of my life to understand that what we see, when we look at another person, may reflect absolutely nothing about how they see themselves. Always having been a woman of size, I have always believed that it must be just a wonderful experience to be thin. What I am learning is that the reverse of the old truism is equally true: inside every thin woman there is a fat woman just waiting to jump out.

We give that woman entirely too much power over our lives.

We all do.

tales from the duck side

MANY, MANY YEARS AGO when I was just a child, a neighbor girl's parents came to my house and gave me a bag of ducks. I remember the bag, which was a big, brown paper grocery sack, and I remember the anticipatory expressions on the faces of the adults around me. I remember realizing the bag held some form of moving life. And I remember looking inside the bag to find myself the proud owner of six baby ducks.

It would never have occurred to me to transport six baby ducks in a grocery bag. (I am not the least bit anal retentive, but I would have gone directly to the animal transport store and purchased the official Audubon-approved duck crate. I would have paid $50. And I would have panicked had I discovered, a week later, that I now needed to transport six baby rabbits.)

As you can imagine (brown paper grocery sacks being about the same size they've always been), my six ducks were tiny. Ducklings, really. Ducklettes. I remember them as being somewhat fuzzy—sort of pre-feathered ducks—of a loose, barnyard-mongrel genus of duck. The day they became mine they were black and yellow and they made sweet little peeping noises in the bag.

I immediately released them, thus learning very early in life that even very tiny, fuzzy ducks making sweet little peeps can cover an amazing amount of ground in a hurry. My father loped off across the back yard to examine his fine personal collection of chicken wire. We built a pen for my duck herd and my duck herd spent the rest of their lives escaping.

Not entirely without provocation, I admit.

The Peck family (or at least my immediate twig of it) at the time belonged to a small but fiercely protective cat named "Gussie" after the tennis player, Gussie Moran. (Both wore what appeared to be white lace panties.) Shortly after the duck pen was built and the duck herd was incarcerated, Gus strolled through the back yard and heard an unfamiliar chorus of sweet peeps.

She stopped.

One ear swiveled, not unlike a radar dish.

Her whiskers twitched.

She dropped her belly to the ground, and, peering through the blades of grass, she espied a small pen of hors d'oeuvres.

I believe Gus may actually have contributed to the ducks' arrival. Gus had a dark side to her personality—downright nocturnal, really—and she frequently came home with a swelling belly and began building little nests all over the house. She and my mother waged prolonged battles over where Gus would give birth to and raise her new family; my bed, my mother's shoe collection and the clean laundry basket being on the top of Gus's list and the bottom of my mother's. Sharp words were spoken on both sides when Gus decided to consolidate their daycare problems and give birth in one of my younger siblings' bassinet. I raised each and every one of Gus's children as soon as I found them, and—tortured by the idle threats I heard from the adults around me—I was quite passionate about homing all of her kittens. It is entirely possible I gave the neighbor's family a kitten—which, I vaguely recall, immediately walked the three miles back home, so I had to give it up again—which may have been what provoked them into be-ducking me.

We did not count on Gus.

Compressed all but flat, she seemed to flow like liquid toward the duck pen, and she coiled to pounce just as my father began wiring on his makeshift lid.

She refused to speak to him for days.

She gave up motherhood.

She did not eat.

She spent all of her time lying in the deep weeds, her eyes drawing a bead on my ducklings, her body utterly motionless except for the steady switch, switch, switch of her tail.

Every once in a while when she just absolutely could not stand it anymore, she would release a howl of pure rage and charge the duck pen, sending the inmates into a panicked peeping clutch on the far side. Then Gus herself would spend some time extracting various body parts from the holes in the chicken wire and she would retreat to bathe herself from toe to tail as if to say, *I didn't really mean that.*

Meanwhile, the ducklings grew and in a very short time became real ducks. Each one would have required his or her own grocery sack.

My father grew tired of retooling the duck pen and wandered off to construct prisons for woodchucks.

By the time Gus managed to penetrate the duck pen, the ducks were roughly the same size she was and there were six of them. They had done hard time. A pact was swiftly drawn: the ducks would huddle together, quacking in mock terror as they raced in tiny circles around their water bowl, and Gus would hunker down and stalk them but never eat them.

My mother amused herself most of the summer by waiting for people who drove into our yard to rush up and warn her that her cat was stalking her ducks. My father used to sit on the back steps with the garden hose in his hand, and when Gus would get the ducks going, he would blast her. I put my younger sisters in the duck pen to see if they would toddle in circles around the water bowl as well. I believe we all grew as human beings.

The tale ends bitterly, of course. It turned out Gus was not alone when she thought of my ducks as food. My own parents murdered my ducks.

My mother—who gave birth to me, and who devoted years of her life to keeping me from watching the miracle of feline childbirth—cooked one of my ducks and tried to make me eat it. I couldn't eat a bite. And neither could anyone else in my family because months of being herded around the water bowl by the spirit of the Serengeti had turned my ducks into about the toughest birds to ever waddle down the pike. My father claimed he broke a tooth and shot a baleful look at Gus.

Once again, she was visibly pregnant.

eleanor

I LIVE NEXT DOOR to Eleanor. Every morning that I don't go to the gym I see Eleanor and her mother race out of their house, coats, scarves and book bags flying as they scrape off their car, jump in and speed off to wherever it is that Eleanor goes. Sometimes we speak. Sometimes we nod. Sometimes my coat, scarf and book bag are flying as well and we just duck our heads and get on with the going.

Once, back in the fall when my leaves were all piled neatly in the street, waiting for the city to come get them, three little girls daintily rode their pink bikes into my leaf piles in what appeared to be an extremely feminine demolition derby. It was at that time that I realized that unless Eleanor is exactly where Eleanor should be, doing exactly what Eleanor should be doing, I really can't tell which nine-year-old girl is Eleanor. I am a bad adult. While I still do vaguely remember how the world spun around me when I was nine, how none but only the most irrelevant adults could fail to recognize me and my significance to the universe on sight, all nine-year-old girls now pretty much look alike to me.

Several weeks ago I stayed home for three days to nurse an

ailing back, and sometime during that brief respite from work, there was a gentle tap on my door and when I went to look, there stood Eleanor. She had one of those color brochures of inedible candies in overpriced tins that seem to be the staple of education finance, and she inquired very politely, in a hurried and obviously memorized speech, which of these delightful tins I might personally wish to purchase. The simple answer would be "none," but there was the noblesse oblige of neighborliness to consider. I gave solemn consideration to several possibilities until it occurred to me that none of the candy ever tastes quite like it should and I should just pick out the tin I objected to the least. So I did so. I asked her if she needed the money now or later and she said it didn't matter—my order should come in X number of days/weeks/months and she would bring it to me. She thanked me very politely and made her escape.

Eleanor is unfailingly polite.

Some time went by.

I don't remember exactly how much time. I had been taking muscle relaxers when Eleanor sold me the tin and at the time I was lucky to have been able to figure out how to open the door to let her in.

However, as my life clipped along, every morning I would see Eleanor and her mother making their run for the car and it would occur to me that I had not yet received my tin. The tin itself was inconsequential: what mattered was that if I did not pay for the tin there was the chance that Eleanor herself might have to pay for it and I didn't want that to happen. No one should have to finance her own education at the age of nine.

One morning I woke up and the whole world had turned white. I keep a male roommate for just that purpose and I listened a moment and heard the rewarding scrape of snow shovel against cement, but I hurried outside anyway to make it appear that I intended to help him, and while I was scraping off my car,

Eleanor and her mother were scraping off theirs. I was feeling neighborly and expansive so I called across the yard, "Hi—has Eleanor's tin order come in yet?"

Eleanor's mother seemed to stiffen for some reason and she said, "Eleanor will have to come talk to you about that tonight," and she jumped into her car and drove away. It seemed a little abrupt to me, but I reasoned that she might be running a little late, with the snow and all.

Of course I did go home that night, but not until very late, and Eleanor, I'm sure, was in bed.

In fact, I rarely show up at home on any predictable pattern at an hour a nine-year-old should still be awake. And to complicate things, I had started going back to the gym, so I left about an hour and a half before Eleanor left in the morning.

And so it happened that I was in the downtown bookstore the Friday after Thanksgiving. I had gone to pick up some reading material for my father, who has recently survived a double valve replacement and, having never been sick before, has become somewhat testy about the whole recovery process. It is apparently somewhat boring for a fixer/putterer/man-of-action to be restricted to lifting less than five pounds. I had heard rumors that his caretaker turned her back on him for five minutes and turned back to find him leaning over to pick up a bread machine, which, as everyone but my father knows, weighs more than five pounds, and my goal was to find less strenuous ways to amuse him.

As I walked past the calendar rack, I espied a small child and I thought to myself, *There is Eleanor.* However, I only recognize Eleanor with confidence when she is exactly where Eleanor should be and the girl in the bookstore could have been any nine-year-old girl with long light brown hair and an aura of femininity about her that would make Barbie look butch. And the child seemed frozen. Not even her eyelids fluttered. She appeared to be staring at the calendar rack. I glanced there to determine what might be holding her attention so rapt and there wasn't much there to entertain me, much less a nine-year-old. I thought about speaking, but then I thought, *suppose her name is Phoebe and she's never seen you before in your life?*

And so I passed her, like an oversized ship in the aisle.

I found a magazine on lighthouses and the Great Lakes, I found a *Penthouse* (my sisters and I used to spend hours slung over our parents' bed, reading our dad's *Playboy* that he always stashed under his side of the bed. We weren't even supposed to be in their room, but we reasoned that if they couldn't see the magazine, artfully hidden by the edge of the bed, they might know we were up to something, but not exactly what. Like there were a broad variety of possibilities to choose from. *There are my childrens' butts all lined up along my bed, they're obviously reading something. I wonder what they could be up to now?*) I found a delightful book of trivia about the Great Lakes. My Beloved found him a puzzle that actually caught his attention and amused him later when we delivered all of this booty.

I was standing at the checkout, making my purchases, when a small, light-brown-haired child materialized under my left elbow and said, "Um—hi."

Since she appeared to know me, I could only assume I knew her as well. "Eleanor," I greeted her.

"Um—we were going to just buy everyone little gifts."

"What?"

She drew a deep breath—possibly her first since she'd seen me. "I took the book to my Grampa's and I left it downstairs and neither one of us remembered it and it was the last day so we never got to send the order in so we were just going to buy everyone a little gift."

I laughed out loud, somewhat confusing her. "Oh, you don't have to buy me a little gift, Eleanor," I assured her. "It's fine."

She looked doubtful.

"Really," I assured her. "I was just worried you might have to pay for something I ordered." I refrained from telling her I'd never wanted it anyway.

She heaved a heavy sigh, as only a nine-year-old can. "I thought you'd be mad," she admitted.

"I'm not mad," I assured her. "You have a wonderful Thanksgiving."

"Thank you very much," Eleanor said. She appeared thirty years younger, no longer plagued by the weight of the world, and she dashed away.

I thought back on that visual image of the child frozen in front of the calendar rack, thinking desperately *Did she see me? Does she know me? Does she look mad? Do I have to talk to her now or can I just pretend I don't see her?*

It must have taken considerable courage for her to come up to me and admit to me she'd lost my tin order. I would have slunk away and tortured myself with guilt and enemy sightings for weeks, but then, I barely recognize the child when I see her, so I guess we don't need to worry about her role-modeling after me.

chocolate malt

MEMORY IS A TRICKY THING. It is the definition of fiction: it starts with an event or a feeling or a perception, and then it wanders off down the corridors of its author's mind until what eventually emerges is "true" only for the person doing the telling.

I had my very first chocolate malt the afternoon I rode the bus home with Pam Sweet and stayed to play at her house.

We were in kindergarten. Pam's mother invited me. Perhaps Pam invited me, although it seems unlikely because while Pam was a nice enough kid I don't remember that we palled around all that often in school. There were six kids in our class, but I had lived my pre-school life in the company of adults and while most adults loved me, I lacked the requisite social skills to have any friends my own age. I was the social leper of my kindergarten class.

I was an intensely competitive child about everything. I had to be the first on the school bus, I had to be the first in line, I had to be the first child called on, I had to do it—whatever it was—first, fastest, loudest and best. I was driven. I was probably the largest child in my class physically, in part because I was also the oldest, and I was strong, and when my charm fell flat on my peers—and it so often did—I resorted to force. I remember plowing through the line to the bus, just shoving aside anyone who dared to stand in front of me, and having no concept of why that might be wrong, or why anyone else might find it offensive. I was goal-oriented. It seemed a silly complication to allow obstacles to voice opinions.

As a result nobody liked me. Everybody hated me. For lunch I sat by myself on the front steps of the school and ate worms.

It is unlikely Pam Sweet said to her mother, "Mom, there's this gargantuan girl in my class who kicks and bites and shoves and is just obnoxious all day long—and I'm the smallest kid in the class so she's made my life a living hell—can I have her over to our house some afternoon?" On the other hand, I have, in my possession, a photograph of Pam Sweet and, indeed, every other girl member of my kindergarten class, grinning over my sixth birthday cake. Pam has both front teeth missing, although I'm sure I had nothing to do with that. Perhaps I was invited to her house as social reciprocity.

Pam Sweet had a playhouse of her very own.

She had a little brother, so her life could not have been perfect, but she had this beautiful, immaculate, physically independent playhouse in the back yard where she could go and be anyone she wanted to be. I asked her what sort of games she played in her playhouse, but I don't recall her answer was particularly satisfactory. I believe Pam was a textbook girlchild of the fifties. She played with dolls and she played house and she had a tea set. I suspect she did not have imaginary friends. She appeared to be confused when I told her what an excellent jail her playhouse would make. None of this may be true, of course, but I do remember having some difficulty finding a suitable game we could play together because hers were silly and she just did not understand mine.

This may be why she took me upstairs in her parents' room and asked me if I wanted to look in their dresser drawers. This seemed odd to me. I had the most territorial mother in the five nearest states, and What Is Mine Is Mine and You Stay Out was the number one rule in my household. I remember her offering the opportunity about the same way she might later ask her guests if they wanted a cup of coffee, as if it were something all of her friends did and she was extending the invitation to me as a good hostess. I may have done it, but my instincts are that I would have declined. I had been told to be good and rifling through someone's mother's things was most definitely Not Good.

I am not sure how well the rest of my visit to Pam's house went. I have no recollection of doing much of anything except discussing her mother's dresser drawers and looking at her playhouse.

That afternoon I spent at Pam's house was probably in the spring. I have a very pungent memory of dampness in the air, that faint green scent about everything, the insistent feeling of buds popping out and things rustling underneath the ground. It may have been the day the Dairy Queen opened.

At any rate, her mother loaded us up into the car and we drove to town (something of an adventure for me, at the time— my mother did not just frivolously "go to town") to the Dairy Queen, where I had my very first chocolate malt.

I have a tendency to sigh while sucking down a chocolate malt, the kind of sigh I have discovered myself giving at other times in my life having absolutely nothing to do with food. I think chocolate malts are God's most perfect food and I've believed that from the first taste of the first malt I ever had. I was nearly orgasmic over this malt.

It occurred to Pam's mother, sometime during this incredibly pleasurable experience of malt drinking, that I had never had

chocolate malt

17

one before. Which I had not. This seemed to tell Pam's mother something, and while I was not entirely sure what it told her, I began to feel like a little backwoods ruffian in the company of society folk. Her attitude toward me seemed to shift, from a sort of reserve to a kind of she-can't-help-it, she-doesn't-know-any-better mien that I did not find at all comfortable. I felt as if I had somehow been disloyal to my mother. I should somehow have arranged to have had a chocolate malt before, so I could have been more prepared for my trip to the Dairy Queen.

I mentioned this later, after I had been taken home, to my mother.

It became clear to me, at the age of six, that Pam's mother and my mother were not friends and never would be. Pam's mother was a social climber, I was told. We were not "good enough" for her. I should not take anything she said or did all that seriously because she was a "snob" and my mother was sorry I had had to go through an experience like that. What I remembered of that experience was a chocolate malt, which I was not even remotely sorry for having gone through, so perhaps some of that conversation was lost on me.

I was never invited to Pam's house again. Later a classmate told me this was because I went through all of her mother's drawers and her mother found me badly behaved. I felt guilty about this for years, although to this day I remember standing in Pam's mother's room while Pam, the eternal hostess, is asking, "Do you want to . . . ?"

Pam and I may have become bored with each other. She was a wonderful girl—I am sure my mother would have been proud to have had a daughter like Pam—but she and I had very little in common. I always liked her, all the way through school, and I made a point of speaking to her at least two or three times a year as we passed in the halls. And she was always nice to me, although I always had the impression that whatever I had just said

fat girls and lawn chairs

to her bounced off one of her internal walls. That may not tell you a great deal about Pam.

I still find it interesting that I was accused of a crime—a misdemeanor, at best, but a social crime, nonetheless—and I have never been able to satisfactorily conclude whether or not I did it. Either I did it, or Pam lied, and why would Pam lie? She told me one of our other classmates went through all of her mother's drawers. Perhaps she was not a perfect child, either: perhaps Pam, at six, went through an unfortunate stage when she told stories that weren't true about other people. Perhaps she was covering up her own complicity. I was certainly not the better child, so I am not qualified to judge.

But I can take the same memory, remember being just unreasonably happy, sitting in a car, holding a cold paper cup full of something, and I can taste that something on my tongue and I can identify that taste on sheer memory. Chocolate malt. Mrs. Sweet introduced me to heaven in a cup. Mrs. Sweet didn't have to be my mother's best friend.

obedience

I WAS A SIMPLE CHILD. I don't believe it required any complex thought to understand anything I did. I liked my things where they belonged, I liked my space respected, I liked my little sisters on the other side of my door. I was a Big Sister. I expected to be obeyed.

Recently during one of those intimate, sharing moments that sisters have, the Wee One admitted to me that when I was somewhere else, she would run into my empty room and stand there. Just stand there. From time to time she stole small items she thought were important to me, but for the most part, she just stood there. Apparently it gave her comfort to know she could orchestrate her own death.

I walked through her room as well, easily twice a day, but that was because her room was the hall and both the UnWee and I had to walk through it to get to our own rooms. Neither the UnWee nor I ever stole small items of victory from the Wee One. We never saw any. The Wee One's room looked like Anne Frank's living quarters in 1941. Friends of mine, in transit to my room, used to look around, frown, and say, "I thought you said your little sister lived in this room . . ." The UnWee and I always thought the Wee One was neurotic, but it turns out she was just neat.

Other than sheer geography there would have been no reason for me to walk into the Wee One's room. Five years younger and obsessed with dolls, she had nothing that would have interested me. Even if she did, I would simply have taken it away from her, so this whole stand-in-your-room thing baffles me.

Ha! She's gone somewhere—I think I'll go stand in her room . . .

"I liked to touch your things," she said.

Touching my things is no great challenge; I keep them all out in the middle of the floor where I can find and touch them myself. As a concession to adulthood I bought a dining room table, but it's never added any great challenge to finding my things.

"You know, of course, that if I'd caught you I would have killed you," I remind her.

This just makes her laugh. "You never knew," she says confidently. "You never missed anything I took, either."

This flashes me back to the single seminal episode of sharing that shaped my attitudes toward siblings in general.

When I was very young—I was perhaps seven and a half—my Grandmother Molby decided to move. She had lived in the same house on Michigan Avenue for thirty or forty years and she was not a woman to recklessly waste things, so our entire extended family went through a period of time when we were each quizzed about our needs. Did my mother want or need the doll collection she had when she was five? Did my Aunt Janette have any use for the linen collection? (This may have been multiple sets of sheets, but, knowing my grandmother, it was her set of "good" sheets with the thin spots or holes in the middle. I can only assume that sometime in her life she was thoughtlessly deprived of a cleaning rag and it was never going to happen again. That, or she expected war to break out and injured soldiers to break into her home, looking for suitable bandages.) I chose that wonderful time in my life, when personal possessions were falling from the sky like leaves, to take up collecting keys.

It was a particularly satisfying hobby because the people in my family were savers. My Grandfather Molby had keys to buildings that were no longer on the property. He had keys to buildings that had never been on his property. He had keys to cars that no longer ran, he had keys to locks he had changed. My Uncle Steve, who looked and talked like Paul Newman, was another wonderful source of keys. All I had to do was stand around looking sad and wistful until someone finally noticed and asked me what was wrong, and then say, "(*sigh*) I sure wish I could find some more keys . . ." (I was not supposed to "bother people" by "asking for things.")

By honing both my patience and my acting skills in a few short months I was able to acquire every key my Grandfather Molby had that would not start his car, open a padlock, or lock a building door. I had to get an auxiliary ring. I had a fine collection of thirty-two keys, which I carried around with me almost everywhere I went. I loved my keys. They represented the love of my uncle and grandfather and the stick-to-itiveness of my collecting desires. They were wonderful keys. Some children don't understand the sheer pleasure of owning an object as mysterious, as powerful, and as satisfactorily physical as a key. I, fortunately, was not one of those children.

And neither, apparently, was the UnWee. She would have been roughly four, still a mandatory nap-taker every afternoon. The naps of my younger siblings gave me this wonderful period of time in the afternoon when I was an only child, so I was adamant the nap-rule be enforced even though I knew the UnWee never slept. And my mother should have known this too since years before, the UnWee while supposed to be napping, simply dismantled her crib, patiently removing every small screw in it.

I had important things to do that afternoon, so I stored my

key collection in its rightful place in the middle of the floor of my room where none of my lesser siblings were allowed to tread, and I went off to do my important things.

When I came back my mom sent me to let the UnWee out of bed, so I went to her room and I found her—wide awake—playing with one key.

My key.

One of my keys.

I found the rings.

I found one or two of the miniature license plates my uncle had given me for my key rings.

I found three keys.

The other twenty-nine keys were not in her bed; they were not under her bed; they were not stuck in the ceiling or jammed in the cracks in the floorboards. I shook her blankets; I shook her pillows; I shook her until my mother made me stop—no more keys.

I was outraged.

First of all, I could not *imagine* what a four-year-old could do with twenty-nine keys that a sister of my advanced age could not undo. They were physical objects subject to the laws of the universe—they had to *be* somewhere.

Second, I could not believe my mother. I demanded the immediate and unquestioning return of all thirty-two of my keys.

My mother said—and this is a direct quote: "Perhaps you should have taken better care of your keys, Sherry."

Like it was *my* job to watch my little sister. I argued that the UnWee had no right to play with my keys, that they were my keys and not hers and she could not just go in my room and take anything she wanted.

I got some vague lecture on the unfinished brains and the fuzzy thought-processes of four-year-olds.

I demanded my keys back.

I was told to go stand in a corner until I could control myself.

At that point I was just too through with the UnWee AND my mother, and I stomped out of the house for good. As it happens I did eventually go home again, but things were never quite the same.

My twenty-nine keys were never found. One four-year-old had my key collection—without authorization—for about an hour in a room eight feet wide and twelve feet long, and twenty-nine of the thirty-two keys she stole were never seen again.

I wanted to have her X-rayed, but my mother refused.

Having lost my key collection and much of my faith in humankind, I drew my lesser siblings together at a time when our mother happened to be elsewhere, and I described to them in rich and colorful detail the multiple forms of death they would suffer if either one of them ever stepped foot in my room again.

I must have made quite an impression because even today, while some of us are drifting into our fifties, I will sometimes catch one of them just touching something of mine and then glancing guiltily at me as if to see what I'm going to do about it.

the carpenter and the fisherman

WHEN I WAS A KID, my father and I built a boat. He told me what we were doing, and then for a long time he messed around with a big sheet of paper with diagrams and mathematical formulas on it, and then he spent some time dragging me to lumber yards where we bought a lot of boards, and then he spent even more time measuring and sawing, and then he dragged me AND my mother out to the barn and they spent time laughing and arguing and bending boards and bolting them in place until eventually he had what looked to me like the skeleton of a boat, and then—FINALLY—the important part came. He filled a little oil can with hot oil, and it was my job to squirt hot oil into all of the holes in the boards. He followed along behind me with a bunch of screws and a screwdriver and filled all of my well-oiled holes with screws so my oil couldn't drip back out. Then we varnished the whole thing—I supervised this project—we painted the bottom red and we had a boat. I have a picture of my father, looking like he is about twenty-six years old sitting in our boat. (There appears to be no trace of the oiler.) I was quite bitter to discover later that my father intended to use our boat to go fishing.

I believe I spent most of my youth fishing with my dad. He loves to fish. As is true of most people, if you want to spend time with my dad you often find yourself doing what he loves to do . . . and when I was very young, I wanted to spend all of my time with my dad. But when I was three or four years old, three hours in a boat holding a fishing pole *seemed* like most of my life.

I was not allowed to sing in the boat. I was not allowed to stand up in, or lean over the edge of, or "fidget" in the boat. I was not allowed to catch weeds as we motored past, or say, "Daddy, look at the big bird!" or throw food to the fish or lay down on the floor and pretend I was dead in the boat. I was to sit on the bench in the middle of the boat, utterly still, with my pole in my hands, my bobber in the water and my hook out of my dad's hair. He was particularly testy about that hook. In one expedition, I artfully hooked six bank weeds, a telephone line and his hat. He was peculiarly unexcited about teaching me how to fly fish.

In the lakes around my home, the most frequent prey for fisherpersons were bluegills, pronounced "bluegill" by the locals. It never mattered whether you had one or twenty, they were "bluegill," as in the sentence, "I'm gonna go out an' get me some bluegill." I don't know what color the other gill is. Grammar police are never invited on fishing trips. Bluegill are flat, fish-shaped creatures that wriggle around on the bottoms of lakes. During certain times of the year you can walk down to the lakeshore, gaze into the murky green waters, and in sandy or smallish-rocky places you can see rounded-out hollows about the size of frying pans, which are bluegill beds. If you pick EXACTLY the right time, you will find Mrs. Bluegill building her bed, or Mr. Bluegill protecting her. Recently a friend told me that this is the best time to fish for bluegill because Mr. Bluegill is hyped to protect his expected family from all comers and will snap at anything that hits the water—not because he is hungry, but because he is plagued by an overdose of testosterone. So when our boat set out to sea, my father's thoughts turned to Catching the Big One, while my thoughts turned immediately to Fig Newtons and Necco Wafers.

I imagine there was all kinds of fishing lore my father patiently explained to me possibly a hundred times, but the information appears to have fallen into the same miscellaneous, irretrievable file as how the brakes on my car work. The information I have stored about bluegill is that they are not a big game fish: a small, inattentive child, for instance, could hook a bluegill and sit there on a wooden boat seat for ten or fifteen minutes, speculating how any grown adult could so passionately love such a boring sport, to have that grown adult turn around and mutter, "Check your line." There is also a law of nature which dictates that when small children fish, they can only catch small bluegill; thus, after spending hours of grueling work landing their prey, their fathers will turn around, unhook their trophy catch, and THROW IT BACK INTO THE LAKE. For a while my dad carried a ruler in his bait box and automatically measured every fish I caught, just to shorten my sulking periods.

As I recall, in the summer we got up every Sunday morning before the sun, peed prodigiously, my dad delivered his lecture about no talking, no squirming, no crying, no wanting to go home again while in the boat, we hooked the boat to the back of our car and drove away, leaving Mom home with the babies. This felt exactly right to me. I had never asked for any babies anyway. Mom was never much of a water person, so how she married us has always remained unclear to me. My dad and I spent most of my childhood on the water, and when the babies grew and became more meddlesome, we dragged them along, too. By this time I got to deliver the lecture about no talking, no squirming, no crying and no wanting to go home again while in the boat. I was all grown up and probably all of six by then.

However, since the family had grown, we had to build a bigger boat. I had generously offered to leave my younger sisters at home and bear the burden of taking my father fishing alone, but once again I found myself manning the oil can. Our second boat was bigger. In my mind they were otherwise identical, but this is perhaps because I performed only specialized labor: I leaned against boards that had to be bent and held to make them boat-shaped, and I oiled screw holes. In fact, by this time several of the babies had toddled out to Dad's shop and—in the interests of peace—he spent a great deal of time filling little oil cans with hot oil and dispensing them to eager, competitive carpenters. When we finished the second boat, my dad covered it with a thick white cloth called "fiberglass" and then smeared that with a thick, pinkish gunk that was apparently some kind of epoxy. Then he itched for several days.

We bought a bigger motor for our bigger boat and then my dad built a surfboard, and we took up surfboarding. Our surfboard was a big, flat plank of plywood painted red with both ends of a rope drilled and knotted through the front to form a rope handle to hang on to and a second rope that tied it to the back of the boat. Our surfboard was almost but not quite aerodynamically correct—it worked, but when we fell off, it automatically dove to the bottom of the lake. Once, two neighbor boys and I were all surfboarding together, I was kneeling in front of them and when they fell, the rope caught me behind the knees and tried to take me to the bottom with the board.

I once tried surfboarding on dry land, was attacked by an imaginary wave and fell, pulling the board up over my toe and driving a sliver about an eighth of an inch wide and three-quarters of an inch long into my big toe, just under the nail. My dad tried to pull it out with a pair of pliers, I screamed, my dad turned green, and we all went to the emergency room where initially the doctors tried to treat my dad.

When he retired, my dad bought a fishing boat. It's a Starcraft twenty-two-footer, with a Porta Potti and an inside deck that sleeps at least two. This thing is HUGE. Six people can ride around and fish comfortably on this boat. He uses it to stalk perch on Lake Michigan. He swears to me there really are perch in Lake Michigan.

I take him fishing once or twice a year. Sometimes I just call him up and inform him that a group of my friends have banded together and will meet him on the dock Saturday morning about eleven. This works out well for all of us because he has time to do his regular 6 A.M. fishing and we have time to meander on down to the dock for his afternoon excursion.

After all these years I think he and I have worked out the kinks in our relationship. I never sing in his boat. Now that I am an adult, I am allowed an occasional fidget. Three miles offshore there are no weeds to grab. I can belly-stab minnows, but when he insists we use something he calls "wigglers," which are a pre-historic larval stage of something with way too many legs and beady little eyes, I hand him my hooks and wait patiently. The last time we went fishing I caught his hat, but he seemed to take it well. His thoughts now turn to Fig Newtons and Necco Wafers after all. The trick, it appears, is to bring food.

zen and the art of
tomato maintenance

THE TIME IS COMING. I can feel it in my veins, edging just a little closer with each thaw. Seeds are turning over restlessly in their sleep. Green things are stirring just below the surface. Tiny buds are just beginning to peep up out of the ground.

It is nearly spring.

Time to plant.

Time to work the earth.

Time to visit greenhouses, pick out plants, make my gardening selections. It is nearly time to spend a small personal fortune on those few chosen plants I wish to set out in my new garden and ignore all summer. I only plant between March and May. After that the mosquitoes come out, the weeds get aggressive, the weather gets too hot and it's time to go inside and read—in my yard the planting season is fairly short.

It's a primordial thing: Babycakes sheds, I bury green things in the ground. This is not to be confused with gardening, which is something my Beloved does: she spends all summer watering and weeding, hoeing and bug-picking. Every other day she drags me to her garden to admire her own personal seven square feet of tomato vines. She just sets herself up for failure and disappointment, but my Beloved is sadly, hopelessly goal-oriented. She does nothing for the sheer sake of doing that thing. There is no distinction in her mind, for instance, between buying pots and buying plants to put in pots, or even setting aside time in one's busy schedule to put the freshly bought plants into the freshly bought pots. In my mind these are all separate adventures and may not even take place in the same decade.

An example of the foolishness of her ways comes immediately to mind. Last year she attached me to the end of a rented roto-tiller and had me dragged, bucking and shuddering, back and forth across her seven square feet of truck garden until it was all bright, damp, fresh loam. Then she planted forty-seven tomato plants and set her watch for August. She bought four jars of mayonnaise. She spoke longingly of the day when she could step into her garden, pluck a bright, fresh tomato, slather it with mayo and eat it right there on The Land.

I would never make this mistake because I have no particular fondness for tomatoes. They are better cold than hot, and they are better out of the garden than out of a grocery store, but nothing much changes their overall tomato-ness—and nothing undoes those big, green squishy bugs that come to gnaw on them.

At first, when the tomato damage began to appear in my Beloved's garden, she thought she had been bug-attacked. Stems were breaking. Huge chunks of her not-yet-ripe tomatoes were being stolen.

"Heavy bugs," I mused, observing the damage. "Big teeth, for your average bug."

Every night more branches were broken, more bites were stolen.

She watched one particular tomato grow and begin to color up. She carried a small, emergency jar of mayo with her every time she went to the garden. She would say to me, "Tomorrow, I think—tomorrow that tomato will be ready."

zen and the art of tomato maintenance

And indeed it was precisely tomorrow morning that she went into the seven-square-foot garden, mayo jar in hand, to discover

The Perfect Tomato

Was gone.

Vanished.

In fact, half the vine was missing.

Her garden looked as if Godzilla might have wandered through during the night. "I don't deal with bugs that big," I said firmly as I surveyed the damage. "I think we should go inside until it snows."

"What on EARTH is getting into my garden?" demanded my Beloved. I murmured fond praises of DDT, a perfectly good bug repellent until the Green People got all excited.

Unfortunately, my Beloved is such a person, and sent me to my room to read *Silent Spring*.

"Yes," I said in my own defense, "but look at the kinds of bugs your bunny-hugging, anti-poison wusses have left us prey to. What if this bug gets bored with eating tomatoes? He could start chewing the tires off our cars, or burrow into the house in the dead of night and start gnawing on your mother."

"I don't think this is a bug," said my Beloved.

"I saw the movie," I affirmed. "It's going to take more than orange juice and dish soap to get rid of this Godzilla."

This Godzilla, as it turned out, was a tomato-stealing dish-soap-resistant groundhog.

"You'll have to move," I said morosely. "Nothing will kill a groundhog. Soon he'll start tunneling under your shed."

"I don't have a shed," my Beloved said. "I sprayed him with the garden hose."

"Oh, that's just wonderful," I dismissed. "Now he's going to swell up and turn into a black bear or something. This is what happens when people like you get all carried away with follow-through: if you gardened like me and just bought a bunch of plants, brought them home and let them die you wouldn't be in this kind of trouble."

"You don't have any tomatoes," she pointed out.

Which is true enough, I suppose, but then—neither does she.

d.b. weeest

During my childhood my mother thoughtfully supplied me with two little sisters and then two little brothers, the first arriving when I was 3.5 and the last when I was 12. Every so often, just out of the blue, she would sit me down and very solemnly inform me that I was soon going to have "a new baby brother or sister." Years would pass. My mother would grow larger and more irritable until one day there would be a flurry of activity and she would go away. Word would float back to me that I had once again been sibled. A week or so later my mother and the sibling would come home, vanishing immediately into the bedroom for another week, and my efforts to acquaint myself with the alien would be so riddled with "BE CAREFUL's" that for most of my life I have been convinced babies are spun from glass.

During our adulthood only two out of five of us have reproduced, but those who do, do so fervently, issuing five consecutive 'phews (until, exasperated, I threatened to push the sixth back where it came from unless it was a girl) and one niece. We are all old now, even the youngest among us is stumbling midway through our thirties, and so we found great delight and vicious humor in discovering that the middlemost among us was once again with child. Hovering on the brink of forty-one (barely able to bench press much more than the front end of her car), the Wee One called me during her fortieth week to tell me her unborn was sleeping peacefully with his/her back to the ultrasound and his/her head tucked affectionately under Mother's right lung.

As close as I've ever been to childbirth, it sounded fine to me and I congratulated her. However, it seems the average pregnancy is forty weeks long, at which point the tenant is expected to voluntarily move out—preferably headfirst. Mother and doctor had conspired, to in effect, serve a seven-day notice to quit ("pay me or I'll take you to court"): the procedure was not designed to induce labor so much as to "encourage" it. I was invited to tag along as company while she endured a long and potentially boring medical procedure.

During the first ten hours we spent at the hospital the baby gave in to the constant pressure from the Wee One and rolled into position. There was much feeling around and much animated discussion of the number of cracks that could be felt, and finally we rejoiced that it was indeed a head (three cracks) and not a butt (one crack) that was being felt. The dangerous aspect of the delivery had been averted (breech birth) and my sister had dilated from 1 to . . . 2 I believe . . . which meant we could just quit and go home. The Wee One, her husband and I, the prospective aunt, discussed the pros and cons of inducing labor or going home to watch TV. We had a TV in the hospital, we had 'phews tucked in safe places for the night, we were there anyway, so we decided to go for it. As quickly as she had given birth to her first two, my sister assured me, she would probably have the child before midnight.

At midnight the Wee One was having actual contractions, which she appeared not to be enjoying. She had dilated to 4 (the goal is 10, I learned). She did not appear to me to be doing anything she had not been doing at 2:00 that afternoon, although she did perhaps seem to be enjoying it less, and it occurred to me that we could still probably pack up and go home childless.

At 12:30 my sister's eyes rolled back in her head, her color disappeared, the contractions which had registered numbers like 15 on her monitor were registering 35 and 42, and she stopped talking to us. She dilated from 4 to 10 in one hour, which may rank up there as one of the most intense hours of my life and all I did was watch. At 1 A.M. the nurses began carrying everything that had been in the birthing room out and dragging in an amazing array of trays, tables and equipment. My sister went to live in some other universe, which consisted entirely of breathing exercises and what appeared to be nonstop, agonizing contractions. The nurses, who had been joking around and very friendly before, became very businesslike when they needed to communicate, very unobtrusive when they did not, and they continued to bring in the stunning array of medical equipment. I stood next to the wall next to my brother-in-law and each of us vigorously rubbed one of her knees. I have never felt so utterly helpless in my life. I knew that she was concentrating her energy on pain control and I attempted to avoid distracting her, but for the first time in my life I knew *why* people boil water, or run around the room like Chicken Little—the need to *do something* was so intense I would find myself having to repeatedly check myself from asking her, "do you want me . . . do you want me . . . what do you want me to . . . ?"

At 3 A.M. she leaned forward and released this incredible guttural growl, the doctor said, "Oh, shit," the nurses seemed to snap into the burst of activity, the doctor flew out of the room to get properly dressed, and we endured about three contractions she had to "blow off" without pushing, and then we had the baby. We had the baby so fast that while the doctor was trying to clear her lungs he barely caught the rest of her as she tumbled into his hands.

fat girls and lawn chairs

What I remember thinking at the time: whatever else we as people may be, we are mammals, and as stunning and as awesome an experience as childbirth may be, human babies are born much like kittens and calves (both of which I have seen). In some misguided sense of modesty or propriety, we have become, as a culture, curiously divorced from the sheer physical power of our being. After the cord was cut, while the doctor was still tending my sister, I held my niece. She can't fool me, and there is no spun glass here—she is made of flesh and blood and bone, and no one who witnessed her birth could be awed by how fragile she is. Tiny, yes (8 pounds, 8 ounces, 21 inches long). Helpless, maybe. For now. What awed the aunt of D.B. Weeest, born 01/29/95, was her sheer determination to be born, shoved like a watermelon through a garden hose to emerge bloody, but unbowed, to look around this strange, unfocused new world and to say, "I exist. Feed me."

changing

I was twelve
painfully
self-consciously
in bud

You were
a year or so older
a year or so younger
sprouting
like saplings

You will always be
that age for me, frozen
in that single glimpse of time
when I understood
that boys and girls
were different

when I would have
changed out of my bathing suit

in total darkness,
if I could
while the two of you
shrieked and snapped towels
and flashed each other,
calling my attention
to each other's nakedness
as if your bodies
so new
and changing
were things
of wonder.

threads

MY SISTER—THE WEE ONE—recently offered me a chance to baby-sit. The Wee One is into crafts, specifically quilting and appliqué. She comes by this quite naturally. Our Middle Sister—the UnWee—is an accomplished seamstress who can transform four pieces of lint and a spool of thread into an evening gown. Our mother made all of her own clothes. And the beginning of every school year of our lives arrived just as our grandmother appeared with patterns, various swatches of fabric and those cursed straight pins, measured our growing bodies from stem to stern. She would disappear for about a week and return bearing three to five dresses for each of us. As a child this struck me as absolutely normal, if just a little homespun for my particular tastes. As an adult I am still awed by the sheer industry of that project—as many as fifteen little girls' dresses in seven days is a daunting project. Even I *know* how to sew. I own the tools, and I have an impressive fabric collection, just in case the bumper sticker is true (She Who Dies With the Most Fabric Wins), but somewhere my skills—and interest—die shortly after the purchase phase. I lack the UnWee's fascination with precision and detail (in truth, we were unevenly stirred while in the womb, and I

ABSOLUTELY lack it—she got it all) and I lack the Wee One's manic passion for activity. She cooks, she cleans, she bears small children in a single bulge—and she attends craft shows to sell her wares.

D.B. is now three and a half months old. She has lost that ball-sprouting-twigs look of newborns and now bears an uncanny resemblance to the fairy-tale baby drawn in one of my childhood books. She is a beautiful baby, a statement I can make with no prejudice whatsoever, and she is a beautiful, breast-fed baby, which means she prefers to visit her mother on a regular basis. So while she comes equipped with a fully functioning thirteen-year-old brother, she requires the supervision of someone with either (a) a driver's license, or (b) a deeper commitment to the next generation than I have.

Baby-sitting for D.B. was sheer hell.

Her mother woke her up, fed her and gave her to me before she left. I tucked her into her stroller and lulled her back to sleep with the sound of my snores. We co-napped until about 10 A.M. when her brother got her up, changed her diapers, dressed her, and suggested we might rush to the car while the mood was still good and the weather sunshiny. I did put her in the car seat, and he did gently let me know how to do it better next time. We went to the craft show, where eighty women converged on us, all cooing, "What a BEAUTIFUL baby . . ." and I didn't see her again for an hour and a half. She fell asleep in the car on the way home. I walked into the house, became involved in a phone conversation with a family member whose life is not going well . . . I had less than an hour and a half to go when several thoughts occurred to me at once.

D.B. was not sleeping.

D.B. was not happy.

D.B.—who was not supposed to be hungry until her mother came home—had ALREADY been fed one bottle of interim formula and her brother, who panics even faster than I do, was ready to feed her another.

I was actually going to have to work for a living.

We tried strolling in the stroller, but we were over-strolled. We tried rocking in the rocker, but it didn't fit and we were restless and we had missed a nap while playing with our brother. We wanted (the Least Wee Aunt determined) to sleep, but we were only 3.5 months and we didn't know how.

So the Least Wee and the Weeest sat down on the couch, cuddled up in a blanket, rocked ourselves, and sang Universal Songs of Truth while the Weeest snuffled about the injustice of unfaithful mothers and the Least Wee thumped. We sang the "Butt-Thump Song" (to the tune of "Jingle Bells"):

> Thump your butt, thump your butt,
> Thump your butt all day—
> Thump your butt, thump your butt,
> Thump your butt today (HEY!)

or the "Ooo'sa Pooh Song" (sung to the tune of "Jingle Bells"):

> Ooo'sa Pooh, Ooo'sa Pooh,
> Ooo'sa Pooh all day . . .

("Ooo'sa" meaning "You are" and "Pooh" being a generic shorthand for anything soft and cuddly, like, for instance, a cat. This is Babycakes' favorite song.)

The songwriter's guild hasn't called me yet.

And finally we gave up on complex lyrics and settled for the "Let Me Sleep" song (sung to the tune of "Jingle Bells").

She weighs fifteen pounds. Her head fits neatly under my chin. Her little hands rested up on my shoulders, one reflexively gripping my neck from time to time. She folded up her legs against

fat girls and lawn chairs

my hips and slept tucked up frog-like against me while I rocked her and thumped her back and crooned nonsensical little songs no one else but my cats will listen to.

I found myself thinking about my grandmother and those fifteen little girls' dresses with the double- and triple-stitched seams, the lace, the rows and rows of decorative stitching, the hems we had to stand still for on the stairway while she hung her row of straight pins . . . it was a woman's ritual. The three of us—our mother, her mother and us girls were the only ones there. We were Getting Ready.

I've been thinking about my grandmother—and my mother—more than usual, these past three and a half months. I find myself making mental notes to remember to show D.B. the Sacred M&M's Flower Arranging Ritual my grandmother and I shared. (This ritual involves a flat-bottom dish, multicolored M&M's, and a passionate desire to create flowers out of small pieces of candy.) I'm beginning to understand why so many of the stories my grandmother told me were about her mother, who died before I was ever born. Her stories were threads sewing us all together, one generation after another, exactly as bits and pieces of used experiences come together to make the patchwork of shared memory. This is where you came from. This is what you could become. These are the women who shaped your life. This is how we survive.

# of mites and men

COCKATIELS CAN LIVE to be twenty-five years old," I lectured, which my friend Annie agreed was a significant commitment. She and I both have reached an age when we must stop and consider whether or not we can afford our infant house pets on our Social Security during their old age. "However," I reminded her, "that may not be a problem in my house."

"That's right," she remembered immediately. "And exactly how do you plan to manage a bird around . . . you-know-who?"

I have never owned a bird. Never even considered one. When I was quite young my great-grandmother kept a parakeet named Joey. Joey had a working vocabulary that included "peetie peetie peetie Pete" (she imagined he was infatuated with a cardinal who lived in the hedge), "dirty bird," and a charming repertoire of ear-splitting whistles. I remember two things about this bird: (1) whenever I dropped my guard, he strafed me and flew away with toesful of my hair, and (2) she trained him to hop around on her chest and kiss her on the lips on a regular basis. Joey never seemed to mind this, and, as far as I could tell, quite willingly obliged. Gram had a nasty habit of grabbing unwary great-grandchildren and demanding the same performance from them. I hated it. I didn't have a great deal of respect for the bird. Also, I believe the little buzzard bit me.

I was utterly bird-free until one evening not that long ago when I accidentally strayed into a pet store on my way home from a balanced, home-cooked feast at Burger King. The craze in my office of late had been for dwarf hamsters, and I thought I might visit one and compose a list of reasons why I didn't need one. I was successful. On the way out of the store I passed something called a "playpen," and playing on the playpen was a small parrot-like bird with a tiny crest, a long tail, clipped wings, and no patience whatsoever with human cuteness. He amused himself, therefore, by poising himself on the edge of the "playpen," fluttering his wings madly and leaping to the ground—which caused him to sort of . . . drift . . . to the floor. Once there, he tucked his wings behind his back, leaned forward, and, looking for all the world like a tiny Charlie Chaplin, took off on his own walking tours of the store.

I was enchanted.

I wanted one.

I alerted the store clerk to the fact that one of his $70 birds was walking to Indiana and the clerk smiled at me with the patience and endurance of a young man who might actually have paid $70 out of a store clerk's salary for the privilege of stomping Mr. Chaplin into the carpet. He said, "Really?"

I could see that not only did I wish to own Mr. Chaplin, he needed me.

I visualized Mr. Chaplin moving into my house, escaping from his open cage onto the floor where he would tuck his wings behind his back, lean forward, and march resolutely toward whatever adventure might await him.

In my visualization I then heard a scream of terror, a streak of orange (or black, or black and white) as Mr. Chaplin became a very expensive cat treat—raw squab, perhaps, or Cornish cockatiel—for the Intrepid Hunter.

My macho housemate, Sir Babycakes, has never been outdoors and has single-handedly purged my house of killer flies, poisonous gnats and that bane of all feline existence, invisimites. He has stalked and furiously killed nail holes. Something that I can't even see lives inside the living room lampshades, appearing to mere mortals as nothing but dust motes, but the mighty Babycakes is not fooled. He purges those shades of demons nightly, never shirking, never wincing, and only occasionally howling with rage and frustration when the invisimites burn his tender noseflesh, or toast a whisker in their own defense.

When my sister closed her quilt store she gave me the stuffed bunny that had hung for years over the cash register. I had often admired it, and she had no further use for it. I brought it home and hung it in the corner of my living room where, if I had one, I might hang a bird cage. It looked like a bunny to me. True, one of my nephews pointed out that it was "silly" because it had wings and bunnies don't fly, but I dismissed him as being too literal.

Babycakes spied that winged bunnything, and he said to himself, "bunnymites." To himself he said, "If I leave that thing alone, then next thing I know she'll be bringing live birds in here."

And he slew that bunnymite.

Repeatedly.

I would have to say that bunnymite is as dead as anything made of cotton and quilt batting can get. Once I caught him dragging my again-dead bunnymite between his legs to his condo, like a lion hauling his kill back to his lair.

"Can you do that to an innocent bird?" Annie asks me.

The best image I can conjure is a feline afternoon amusement called "Leaping for Cockatiels," which involves Sir Babycakes vaulting from the couchback to the cage and clinging like a huge, homicidal cover; to be quickly followed by "Bowling for Cockatiels," in which Nicky and Babycakes take turns rolling the bird cage, torn by sheer cat-weight from the ceiling, along the floor from room to room while Mr. Chaplin exhausts himself just trying to stay upright and away from the edges.

It's hard to convince myself this would be more fun than walking behind the pet shop counter and beaking that store clerk on the ankle.

the southwest michigan jaguars

I NEVER WANTED to play football. I never wanted to fight in Vietnam. (I mention that because it was one of the other options not open to women when I was planning my life.) I never spent a minute of my life envying men for their football skills or their ability to get shot, and I ruled out both as possibilities for myself for about the same reasons. You could get hurt. The fans were fickle. There was way too much controversy involved for someone as ambivalent as I was to choose that path.

As far as I know, any woman my age who actually played football did so because she had brothers who were either tolerant beyond their times or trying to kill her. We were allowed to use the gym on evenings six weeks out of the year to play intramural volleyball (if the boys weren't using it). Period.

Later Title IX came along and the quality of men's sports was compromised forever by the odd assumption that girls were entitled to explore as many life options as boys. Apparently now in some schools there actually are women's varsity football teams.

I don't often watch football. It's a brutal sport. Beyond the obvious bumping and slamming on the field, there is me in the grandstand shouting, "Kill him!" or "If you can't outplay him, hurt him." Football does not showcase my best qualities. And the overall camaraderie of the fans has never been quite the same since they made us stop passing the cheerleaders over our heads.

So earlier this spring my Beloved announced our area was developing a women's football team, and we were required to go immediately to the nearest field and wait for them to play.

I said, "Why?"

This was wrong. I should have said, "Oh, great—let's go show our support for women younger, stronger and more determined than we are. Perhaps if we're quick enough, we can carry a wounded one off the field."

Last night my Beloved organized a small group of friends and we attended the first ever game played by the Southwest Michigan Jaguars. They played an orange-and-white team from Detroit. They got creamed 34 to 16. The score, however, is beside the point: they got out there, they played their hearts out, and in the second half they pulled their offense together and got two touchdowns AND a two-point conversion. They stood around and had their pictures taken. They came back to the showers and a crowd of devoted fans who had waited for them. They sold out the seating in the bleachers. It was a good game.

I think if I had ever wanted to play football badly enough to pay $500 just to try out, if I had made the team, if I had practiced my heart out and if I had finally PLAYED FOOTBALL it would have been one of the most glorious nights of my life. It was fun to be a part of that. *Yes. Women really can play full-contact the-same-shit-the-boys-play football. We just did it.*

And this is wrong and I know it and I should be slapped on the hand for even mentioning it, but . . . the number of men who came to watch surprised me. *Are you surprised by the number of women who attend men's football games?* Actually yes, but then, I don't like football. *Do you just automatically assume that no one would be interested in women playing sports?* No—I assume men wouldn't be interested. *So after twenty-five years of identifying yourself as a feminist, you still define your values by what you perceive men to value?* No, I'm just surprised that many men came to see women play football on a Saturday night. And apparently so were the players because the newspaper article I read stressed, every other line, how many husbands and boyfriends were bringing them water and offering moral support. I expected to see thirty men on the sidelines wearing their MY WIFE IS NOT A LESBIAN badge; it was the two hundred men in the stands that surprised me.

We all know, of course, that one of the players got sacked because she "ran like a girl." (In fact, I don't believe that criticism came from a man.)

When the ball carrier for the Jaguars ran for the first touchdown a Detroit player came barreling in from the side and smacked dead-on into a well-set Jaguar guard, bounced off and landed on her butt in the grass and the man behind me went crazy. "Did you SEE that? My God, that was one hell of a block!" All around us amazed male voices decreed, "That was a good play!" Two plays later the man behind me turned to his companion and said, "Yeah—but did you see that block back there? I mean, she just WHOMPED her . . ." (I'm not really making fun of the boys. It really was a textbook block and I was pretty impressed myself.)

Several things impressed me, even in spite of my abysmal ignorance of the game. In about the middle of the front line was a woman who appeared, from the stands, to be shorter and smaller than most of the other players. The quarterback would snap the ball, all of the players would begin running, they would all bunch up in the middle and fall on the pile, and then they would start unpiling until there was only the smaller woman left, and each time she would spring up like a Timex watch and get in line to do it all over again. She must be made of Teflon-covered rubber.

fat girls and lawn chairs

Oh, yes—football is a team sport. Another reason I never wanted to play football was I never did well at team sports. To play team sports well you need years and years of practice of keeping track of not only what you are doing, but what everyone else on the field is doing and how what each of them is doing impacts on what you should do next. Volleyball is the most complex team sport I ever played and when I played you had your own sacred little patch of land and you played it come hell or high water. To play team sports well, you need a sense of camaraderie among your fellow players, a sense of higher purpose and willingness to trust that your fellow teammates will step in and cover you when you fail, back you up when you need it, even a willingness to sacrifice yourself for the good of the whole . . . all that T-word (trust) stuff. That's what boys learn and have always learned on the playing field where girls were forbidden to go.

Girls don't learn the rules of engagement. Girls don't learn the difference between personal victory and team victory or personal loss and team loss. Girls learned that if you don't do it yourself, it doesn't get done. Girls were never asked to fight the war in Vietnam or any other war. But if they had been, girls would have won. Girls would have felt guilty for not winning it sooner, and girls would have restored all of the roads, rebuilt all of the bombed homes, adopted all of the orphans, established daycare centers, domestic violence shelters and homeless shelters, and girls would have processed endlessly about what we could have done to have prevented the war and what we still can do to prevent it from ever happening again. Because girls believe, in the end, everything that happens is our own personal fault.

To avoid having personal fault for a Jaguars loss, our gang drove immediately to the Meijers' store—our team's sponsor—to buy team Ts and team paraphernalia. Sadly, there were none to be had. I presume we will be sewing our own. My Beloved is thinking of giving the team mascot a gift certificate to a massage therapist to compensate for balancing that costume head all night. We have preparations to make. First, we need to find a schedule because—although we are pretty sure we have four more home games this season—we don't know when any of them are. To build up our cheering voices, we have all vowed to practice shouting "Go Deeper!" each morning in the shower. So if you hear any odd shouting before the next game, that's what it is.

eminent domain

IF YOU WALKED OUT the back door of my parents' house, drifted on past the old garage with its charred back wall and the cement foundation for the larger building that burned away, and on past the converted henhouse where my father kept all of his tools (and himself much of the time) you would come to the end of my yard. My yard ended more dramatically than most people's—it dropped, almost vertically, about twenty-five feet into a big, green pond. The view to the left of the back pond was more picturesque, but no less startling: the little green pond was surrounded by a willow woods and when I was young, it hosted a small school of rogue goldfish that would float up to the surface and speckle the dark water with splotches of white and gold.

A few years ago my nephew misnavigated and rode his grandfather's four-wheeler headfirst over the bank into the little green pond. His little brother rode right along behind him. The pond is nowhere near as deep as we presumed it was when I was a kid. My father, the Groundskeeper, had spent a great deal of time eradicating "weeds" (anything not a maple) from the bank, so it must have been a short, fast ride, just about long enough to let nine years of sin flash before the child's eyes. Then his grandfather burst over the bank, tore down the hill and—every instinct tells me—gave a remarkable demonstration of the famous Peck temper. Both boys survived without a scratch, discounting injuries to the ego. The four-wheeler, remarkably enough, lived as well, but it took my father most of the afternoon to haul it back up the bank and it was some time before my nephew so much as acknowledged the cursed vehicle again.

Both ponds were part of the huge kidney-shaped hole surrounding our yard we called The Gravel Pit. We spoke of it quite definitively—The Gravel Pit—as if it were the only one, as if no one else in south central Michigan had ever seen or heard of one. It was large and fairly irregularly shaped and both my yard and my best friend's, around the corner, were chipped out of it. From fence post to fence post of the fields that contained it, it was about a quarter of a mile wide at its widest point, and it was a little longer than it was wide. Ours was unconventional by most gravel pit standards: it hid the Great Plains, a section of Death Valley, the North Woods and an extraordinary number of wicked and untamed Indians (for, I fear, it was a politically incorrect gravel pit). I hunted both buffalo and Jesse James there in my youth.

On rare occasions huge dump trucks would roar down the drive and haul away parts of our universe, something I believe all of us who hunted and foraged there considered to be both unnecessary and downright rude, but the intrusions were rare. Much of the imaginary landscape was based on the topography—there were real trees and even a small woods (serendipitously to the north) and most of the pit was carpeted with weeds and wild grass.

When the dump trucks came, we retaliated by laying our rocks in complex and mysterious patterns to frighten the intruders away. (Imagine their surprise. "Sorry, Boss, but we can't go down there anymore—those kids have been laying our rocks again and—frankly, sir—we're scared.")

We were powerful.

Gravel pit rocks were particularly powerful.

The gravel pit was all the more fascinating because we weren't supposed to go there. It was dangerous. Bad things could happen to us down there—things our mothers might not discover for (my mother's favorite measure of time) *God Only Knows How Long*. There was a magical shield that protected us from maternal mind-reading rays while we were down there. That prospect alone was enough to drive me over the edge at the slightest excuse.

The total count varied, depending on where the occasional cranes did their digging, but most often there were three ponds (the third pond was not visible from our yard), each over sixty feet deep. (We never actually measured them, but there is no point in having a pond less than sixty feet deep, since you will always lose the "my pond is deeper than your pond" debate.) There was the big green pond, the little green pond and the hole. The hole was spring-fed and maintained a toe-tested temperature of 32 degrees year-round. We swam in the hole once by accident. Five or six of us just slipped and fell in. Any of the ponds were dangerous swimming because they were just holes full of water dredged out by the big metal buckets on the cranes and the bottom could be anywhere at any time. The most accessible bank of the hole went from an inch to over six feet deep in less than three feet and the bottom was gravel, so it was significantly easier to fall in than to fall back out again. While we were in, however, we spent a great deal of our splash time challenging each other to touch bottom since the water only two feet below the surface was all but unbearably cold, and when we did scramble out, we came out blue. Normally we were not allowed to swim in the ponds because they were "stagnant," a word my mother dismissed as meaning "dirty and full of diseases." We used to peer into the water and look for diseases, but the worst thing I ever saw was a crayfish, which looked like a miniature bleached lobster. When one of my little brothers fell into a pond, we all cheerfully promised him he was going to turn stagnant and die.

The gravel pit grew some of the healthiest, lushest, greenest poison ivy I have ever seen. It grew like a pampered English ground cover. My best friend and I (and several annoying younger siblings) discovered a particularly satisfactory patch of wild grass once and conducted an adventure I can no longer recreate, but it involved a great deal of rolling around in all of this lovely grass. Grasshoppers may have been involved. I went home and had dinner; she went home and had herself admitted to the hospital for a week with poison oak over 90 percent of her body. I never grew a bump. She got to miss a week of school: I got quizzed about how I managed to lure all of my innocent younger siblings back into the deepest corner of the forbidden Pit of Iniquity where I could deliberately expose them to life-threatening weeds.

I was not particularly fond of my innocent younger siblings—they followed me everywhere, even in the face of the vilest threats, and they frequently resorted to the innocent sports of blackmail, extortion and coercion to include themselves in matters that were none of their business—but the sad truth is, I still don't know what poison oak looks like. And neither do my innocent siblings because—of course—not a single bump arose on their thick little hides either. My best friend and her brother scratched and dug and molted for weeks. (There were three of us girls, all perfectly healthy; two of them, in misery. Their mother never looked at us girls quite the same way after that.) Fortunately, my baby brother was too young to have followed us on this adventure. He has to take cortisone shots just to stand in our back yard without scratching and whenever they sense him coming, you can still find the fine young tendrils of poison ivy snaking up on the lawn to find him, not unlike *The Day of the Triffids*.

Each spring the snow would melt and much of the floor of the pit would be flooded. As early summer approached, the water would begin to evaporate and there would be massive pools of black commas left to writhe and die in the sun. I could not imagine that mother nature would be that wasteful and for years I would drag my best friend down there and, armed with our trusty mayonnaise jars, we would spend literally hours scooping up stranded tadpoles and carrying them to the safety of deeper water. It is possible that a million frogs owe their lives to us.

I remember all of this as if it were what was important to me at the time. It wasn't. When I was a kid, the gravel pit was my domain. It was where I went to be alone, the world I could control. There were times when I barely tolerated the company of my best friend, much less that of lesser beings. I spent hours walking back and forth, retracing the same steps along the same path over and over again while I wrote spectacular adventures in my head about truly exciting people who lived extraordinary lives. One of the small ironies of life, perhaps, is that those stories, which utterly consumed me at the time, were stories invented by a child to entertain a child and would probably not make a great deal of sense to me now if I could remember them. The minor things—the time that I spent with my friends and my family—those are the things that I now remember.

what she lost

When her breasts
betrayed her
with cancer
she had them
removed

lopped off

returning,
at the age
of fifty-five
to those tit-free
scorching
days
when she ripped off
her shirt
and ran
bare-chested
through the heat
as careless as any boy

"So how does it feel
to be flat-chested?"
we ask
and she grins:
and for a minute

we all remember.

wounded in action

I HAVE A SOFTBALL INJURY. I expect it will be quite impressive in a day or so—it is barely three hours old now and it has made its presence known. In the center is a white oval, surrounded by an angry red ring something like a bull's-eye (can you catch Lyme disease by playing softball?) which is, in turn, surrounded by a lavender bruise. But because even I have a little pride, allow me to explain WHY this injury occurred before we get into exactly HOW.

I don't play softball. In fact until this summer I could honestly say the last time I watched a softball game I was—give or take—ten. However, my cubiclemate plays and this spring she had to switch teams and I went along—once—to offer a little moral support. Until then I had assumed a softball game would last three to seven hours and would require an audience of several thousand people. Having gone once, I was pleased to discover this gesture of moral support was a sacrifice of barely an hour of my time and was actually kind of fun. I went again. I got to know a few of her teammates by name. I've gotten quite comfortable, going to watch Cathy's games. I root. I cheer. There are six or seven of us hard-core Robin's Roost fans and we have our own secret handshake by now.

I know when to shout, "Good eye."

These things are important.

So I was innocently seated in my fan seat, waiting for my team to arrive, when Cathy snuck up behind me and accused me of rooting for the men who just happened to be on the field at the time. I quickly explained that I was early. She and I then observed that men seem to continue to play softball much longer than women do. And then we both admired the irony that Cathy, who is thirty-eight, is the oldest player on her team.

Her team had not yet arrived.

As game time approached, they began counting themselves. I smiled and rooted, since I have never had any particular reason to count how many players there are on a softball team. I was smiling and rooting for no one in particular when Melissa, the team captain, turned to me and said, "Do you want to play?"

In the movies this moment is always the climax of the plot—that Golden Moment when the Kid Who Always Wanted to Play has her chance to play with the big girls. In the movies she has her cleats on her feet, her glove in her hand, a spare ball in her hip pocket, and she jumps up and down and cries, "Oh, man, Coach—just give me a CHANCE!!!!" I said, "Yeah, right," and rooted for someone in the distance.

They were all still looking at me. There were not enough of them. If I refused to play they would have to forfeit the game. I looked left. I looked right. I offered to try to bribe a player from the other team to defect. I looked down at my own self to determine if something movie-like and magical had happened when I wasn't looking.

I am forty-six years old. I am five feet seven inches tall, I weigh three hundred pounds (plus change). I do not run. I do not catch. I do not throw. I gave up playing with balls when I was ten. I have never actually stood on a softball field before. I said, "Get real."

They said, "If you don't play, we can't play either."

I said, "I can't catch, I can't throw, I can't hit, and I can't run. Other than that, I'm damned good."

They said, "You can play right field."

I believed, in the confusion of the discussion, that I was agreeing to play until my replacement arrived, which—I believed—meant I would walk out onto the field, my replacement would drive up, I would be shooed off the field and thanked profusely for my space-taking abilities.

So I was given a glove, someone suggested I try putting it on my LEFT hand, someone threw a ball at me twice (which I assume someone fielded) and I was herded out to right field. It seemed safe enough. I waited for my replacement to arrive.

My replacement arrived.

They put her in center field.

They continued to play.

I was still on the field.

My cubiclemate—who plays catcher—began calling my name and insinuating something about left-handed batters, everyone on the team became immensely interested in my personal space-taking skills, and the batter, who was standing backwards on the plate, connected with the ball and arched the specious little orb

over the first basewoman's head

and right at me.

The first basewoman called, "Cheryl, you got it?"

And I answered, "Hell, Noooooo . . ." And I raised my big, clumsy mitt in the air, and I ran toward that vicious, nasty little ball as it snubbed my mitt altogether and smote me in the middle of my outstretched arm—nearly breaking it, I might add—and then bounced . . . off into the boondocks, somewhere . . .

My one claim to fame as an outfielder, and I have a big purple stain on my arm that says, "Next time: BIG barn, b-r-o-a-d side. . . ."

fat girls and lawn chairs

I thought I was safe the other half of the inning. I thought, *they know I can't hit, so they'll run a sub for me*. Obviously I didn't think this through: if they'd HAD a sub for me, they would have put her in right field. So I found myself at home plate with a bat in my hand and a woman not far enough away throwing balls at me. I was thinking one thought as I held my bat. I was thinking, *If you hit this, you have to run*.

Run.

I haven't run since 1962.

I thought a comforting thought: I thought, *What are the chances . . . ?*

I swung my bat.

The stand went wild. My team went wild. Everyone in south central Michigan was yelling, "Cheryl, R-U-N . . ."

So I gathered every fiber of my being—and there are many, many fibers in my being—and I pointed them all toward first base, and I leaned in that direction, hoping to add speed at a later date, and—although in my heart and soul, I was running— I . . . drifted . . . with the grace and delicacy of perhaps a hippopotamus . . . toward first base.

For reasons unclear to me, I was safe.

They had several years to throw that ball across that plate, but apparently they threw it somewhere else.

I was given instructions: if the ball went into the air I could wait, but if the batter hit it at the ground I had to run immediately. The batter hit it at the ground and once again I gathered, motivated and lumbered on down the road. I reached severe oxygen deficit at second base. I was breathing like a freight train. The field, which had looked small from the stands, had grown several miles in its overall proportions. It was 94 degrees and humid. It occurred to me that I could get to third faster in an ambulance than on foot.

The next batter hit the ball. Once again I ran. The stands

wounded in action

were going wild. I sensed my entire team running each step with me, as if willing me on. I was waiting to be tagged or crippled or tripped . . . but I arrived on third (AGAIN) safe.

I knew this time I was the one they would kill. I knew they'd be lucky to kill me before I ran completely out of air and just expired six feet short of the plate. The batter swung, the batter hit, I lumbered slowly and loudly over home plate . . . to discover the opposing team had tagged their third out on someone else on another base and my run didn't count.

Furthermore, I had to go back to right field and wait for more ball attacks.

I did make it up to bat again, and I actually hit the ball—sadly, right at the pitcher, who scooped it up and sent it to wait for me at first. As I was shambling back to my team, someone on the opposing team remarked, "Well, you made it across home plate last time. . . ." I wasn't sure how to take that, so I smiled and shambled on.

In retrospect, I've decided to take it as a compliment. My team, inspired by my spirit and mastery of the game, may have set a new league record with our score of 25–2 before the mercy rule kicked into effect and they let us go home and—while it had nothing to do with anything I did—I was one of the few runners on my team to come anywhere near home plate.

But I think I'll hang up my glove. Or whoever's glove it was. There has never been a single moment in my life when I found myself thinking, "Gee, I wish I were playing softball right now," and I expect even fewer in the future.

And—just for the record—that ball isn't soft.

the designated fetcher

When I was very small, my dad was the coolest person on earth. He may still be—when I was a child, he lived right there in my house and all I had to do to be near greatness was go outside and listen for the sound of work being done.

My father was always working. About ten years ago he retired, which has given him more time to concentrate on the home repairs, yard work and carpentry of his extended family. He carries a small notebook where he stores the exact dimensions of my Uncle Don's cottage bathroom, how many board-feet of lumber he needs to finish his friend Toby's back steps and the exact style of ceiling tiles we need to redo my kitchen. This work ethic courses through my family and it coursed right past me.

When I first became an adult, I used to invite my dad over to my house. We would sit around, struggling to make small talk. Sooner or later I would ask him how to fix something and seconds later we would be gathered around that thing, eyeing it, measuring it, evaluating it, taking notes about dimensions and required tools and materials in his notebook. Over the years I have eliminated a few steps. Now I call him up and say, "Dad, my toilet doesn't flush right—what time would you like dinner?"

I have no real gift for work, myself. I am tool-impaired. I have yet to hit the same nail twice with a hammer. I can drill holes in the wall with a screwdriver and I once peeled the skin off my knuckles with an electric drill. I like tools—particularly power tools—but I rarely have the opportunity to actually own any. I mentioned once to my dad that I was enchanted by a small chain-saw and the next day I heard a familiar roar and found him in my front yard, buzzing every tree I owned into kindling. I am not allowed to own a circular saw, either; something about cutting off my own leg. "Those things will kill you," my father decrees and locks his shed in case I might wander in in my sleep.

I am better than I used to be.

As a child I was my dad's designated fetcher. I would be innocently basking in the glow of his greatness when he would say, "Run out to the barn and get that 3/8ths wrench on the middle bench next to the drill press." It broke my heart. I wanted to be with him and I spent most of the time I was with him being sent away. These missions I was sent away on rarely enhanced my standing in my father's eyes.

Shamefully I must admit how easily the worm can turn: I just woke up one day in the middle of performing some task for which I did not have the right tool—although I knew exactly where the right tool was—and I looked up and there, lingering aimlessly right near me, was a small, mobile being, and it just seemed so natural to me to say, "Hey kid—run down in the basement on the bench by the dryer and get my vise grips and the blowtorch. . . ."

I was a lazy child, but my greatest objection to being the designated fetcher was that I could never find what I had been sent to fetch. I could find the shed. I could find the middle bench. The middle bench—like the right bench and the left bench—was home for many of my father's tools. There were grinders and polishers and twisters and benders. There were screwdrivers with flat noses and screwdrivers with star-shaped noses and nutdrivers that only looked like screwdrivers. There were hammers and mallets and sledges. There was the thing he used to beat his tires with and the thing he used to make the tires get off the wheels with and the thing he used to tighten the spokes on my bike. There were jars of bolts and washers and screws and nails and nuts and brads and staples, and there were drawers of hinges and fasteners and drawer pulls and latches and locks. There were machines with blades and machines with drill bits in them and machines with sandpaper and one of these machines—and only one—was called a "drill press."

I had never pressed a drill.

I had no idea why anyone would need that done, much less what the machine that did it would look like.

The problem, of course, was that if I couldn't find the drill press, I couldn't find the 3/8ths wrench next to it.

I would eventually admit defeat, but I rarely went immediately back to my dad for further instructions because it always seemed to make him mad. So I would linger in his shed, studying his girlie posters, or perusing his tool chests, just taking notes in case I might later be sent to find something in one of them (he had four). Eventually I would wander back to my dad and I would say, "(*sigh*) I can't find it."

"Did you look on the bench?"

"Unhunh."

"Did you look next to the drill press?"

Could be. Maybe. How would I know? "Unhunh."

"And it wasn't there?"

And maybe it wasn't. Maybe I couldn't find it because it wasn't there to find. I could wriggle right off the hook, here. "Nope."

He would think. He would frown. "Are you sure?"

I would be, by then, very very sure the wrench was nowhere

near that drill press. He had lost his wrench and was sending me on a wild goose chase, and he could not possibly blame me for that. "I'm sure," I would say.

He would use bad words. He would stand up and stalk out to the shed as I tagged along like a kite tail, and he would walk into the shed, up to the middle bench, next to the machine with the drill bit hanging out of it, and he would pick up his 3/8ths wrench and show it to me. He would say, "It's right here."

"It wasn't there when I looked for it."

"So why would it be there now?"

I would have no idea how that could happen, but personally I always blamed it on the red squirrels. My father hated red squirrels, anyway.

"So what were you doing out here all that time?"

I was not a stupid child. I knew, even at a tender age, that the answer to that question is not *I thought you would yell at me so I hung out for a while*. I've never been entirely sure why that is a wrong answer, but it is.

So I would answer, "I was looking."

"But it was right there," he would say, and walk off, shaking his head.

Over time he came not to believe me the first time I came back empty-handed. He would repeat his instructions and send me back. My dad has a very soft voice and very little patience with repeating himself, so I learned, as a child, to memorize vocal patterns and just repeat them, over and over again in my head, until I could translate them into standard English. I don't hear any better than anyone else, but I am of invaluable aid to people watching home movies with mushy soundtracks.

Still, there was one other small problem with going out to the shed to the middle bench right near the drill press for the 3/8ths wrench. I could never tell his wrenches apart.

He had numbered them all through some vague system that

eluded me. He had a 3/8ths wrench, a quarter-inch wrench and a half-inch wrench, all of which I spent my childhood looking for. I learned to distinguish one from another because the 3/8ths wrench had a nick in the handle part, and the quarter-inch wrench had a chunk of white paint on it, and the half-inch wrench was bigger than the other two. But all three were whole wrenches, not 3/8ths of a wrench, or half a wrench, and all three were several inches long. I was an adult before one day I noticed they had little fractions embossed on the handles that appeared to be about the width of the mouth of each wrench.

What a handy little piece of information that could have been.

Still, I never ran out of things to talk about with my dad.

What are you doing, Daddy?

What does it look like?

Where did you say it was again?

I'm looking for it.

staring at the light

HIS MOMMY IS PLAYING with the light machine again. She is not down in the kitchen, stirring Babycakes' food. She is not sleeping on the couch where a tired young man could curl up and take a nap. She is sitting in her chair, staring intently at the light. From time to time she wiggles her fingers around the board, making funny little clicking noises, and other times she just stares. Babycakes has no idea what she finds so fascinating about the light. Sometimes when he stares at it little things move around inside and he slaps them. This makes Mommy laugh. Mommy never slaps the light machine. Hardly ever. Sometimes the light machine talks to her just like a Big One and says things like "You have mail" or "did you PAY for a Gateway?" Sometimes Mommy talks back to the light machine, and says things like "Give me my file," or "Out of memory THIS, you pile of junk," but she never chases the moving thing, which leads Babycakes to think he will never, never understand Big Ones.

Mostly the light machine is a severe annoyance for Babycakes. Mommy won't let him sleep on the clickboard. When he jumps up to see her, Mommy mutters, "I can't see the monitor" and puts him back down on the floor again. This could be a nice game but then Mommy gets all mushy and tries to hold him and then he has to poke her again . . . Once he had to poke her and she put him out of the room and shut the door!!!! Babycakes was so angry he had to cry. He had to lie on his side and fish his paw under the door. He had to step back and YOWL about how angry he was, locked outside a room where he had every right to be and where Mommy was that very moment . . . Gypsy came to the door to see why he was angry and immediately discovered she was on the Wrong Side of The Door too, so she cried, and finally Mommy came and said, "stop this," which is Mommy's way of saying, "I'm very sorry I upset you, little Babycakes, and I will never lock you out again." Once he was safely back in the room again, Babycakes was still so angry he had to sit with his back to Mommy and twitch his tail, just to punish her. It was a dark day, indeed.

When he needs his rest, Babycakes likes to climb right up on top of the light box and sleep. It is very warm there and just the right size for a fine young cat. If he's in a particularly good mood, he can look down at his Mommy and give her a slow, approving blink. This rarely happens, however, because Mommy is always messing with his tail. If Mommy wanted a tail to play with, she should have grown one of her own. Babycakes can't imagine life without a tail anyway. Sometimes he finds it hard to respect Mommy. No tail. No coat. No tail . . . But there she is, murmuring, "I can't see the monitor, Cakes," and messing with his. Often she irritates him so much he is forced to go sleep on the platform.

The platform is really the best place to sleep anyway. It is raised, so one eye can catch a clear view of the room. It is away from the clickboard, where Mommy once yelled and called him a "cursed thief" or "cursor thief." (Who knows what Mommy says? She talks all of the time. She walks in from where the air changes and says, "I'm home, Babycakes" like she expects him to say "Oh, goody-goody, Mom . . ." She doesn't even have a tail to flick, to show how silly an idea that really is.) Sometimes when she is staring at the light, Mommy does something to the platform—Babycakes knows she does—and completely without warning it will jump to life, making all kinds of screeching noises which fray Babycakes' nerves. It has never done this to him when Mommy is away.

But he is not without revenge. When Mommy spends too much time staring at the light . . . when his box is bad, and his food is old, and no one has stroked his fur or rolled a ball for him to play with—just in case he feels like playing—he knows exactly what to do. He walks into the light room. He looks around. He flicks his tail. He opens his mouth, and he YOWLS. And he walks out of the room.

Once when Babycakes was very young, he became sick. He spent hours in his litterbox trying to do what should have taken a matter of minutes, and this frustrated him, so he went to Mommy and told her how unhappy he was. Mommy put him in a box and took him to Mr. Needles. Mommy said, "I have no idea what's wrong with him, but he won't shut up." Mr. Needles poked Babycakes with a series of pins and charged Mommy many, many dollars (a deal Babycakes could see was rotten from the word "go," but . . . she has no tail.) That happened nearly all of his life ago (well, it happened three times nearly all of his life ago) and now whenever Babycakes cries, Mommy stops whatever she is doing and comes to talk to him about his "feelings." She rubs his tummy. She asks him about his box. Mommy can get downright sappy, truth be told, but she stops staring at the light.

This, in catspeak, means "power."

black holes

IT IS ONLY RECENTLY that I joined the ranks of the socially responsible. Before that I lived in an apartment, worshipped regularly at the Laundromat of my choice, and my major appliance was an electric typewriter. It was during this time that I knew my friend with the black hole in her basement.

My friend loved clothes and she loved to dress . . . distinctively. Her wardrobe was the talk of the office and even the clients occasionally picked her out as "the one with . . ." (and we would finish "funny clothes?" We were sensitive). The thing that impressed me most about her wardrobe was that nothing in it ever seemed to live more than three or four months. She bought six outfits for every one that I bought, but she never had anything to wear. I would ask, "Whatever happened to that cute little . . . ?" and she would answer, "I can't find it."

I had exactly enough clothes to survive fourteen days, and I went to the Laundromat every two weeks. I hauled every piece of clothing that I owned into the Laundromat, washed them, and then hauled them back home again, and in twelve years of Laundromatting I never lost a sock. My friend lost entire OUTFITS and she did all her own laundry in her own washer and dryer in her own basement. "Where," I would question patiently, "could it go?" and she would answer, "You just don't understand—you don't have any kids." I believed her. For years I believed her.

One evening I went to her house and accidentally stumbled into her basement. In her basement was a pile of clothes—not three towels, a sock and a pair of jeans—a pile of clothes roughly six feet high and eight feet wide, a virtual monument of clothes, a Symbol of Something as esoteric and as hard to overlook as the humming monolith in *Space Odyssey 2001:* and when I asked her what it was, she said, "Oh—that's just stuff." I just gaped in awe. A sneaking suspicion tormented me, but I managed to refrain from drawing any reckless conclusions about the black hole that regularly swallowed her wardrobe.

Time passed.

I bought a house. With the house came a basement. I stood in my new basement, gazing around at all the empty space, and I said to myself, "I'll never be able to fill up this basement."

Because I had a basement I bought a washer and a dryer.

This evening I went to my closet and discovered that an entire set of flannel sheets had escaped. They were MIA. I don't take my sheets to work. I don't take my sheets to the Y. I haven't been to a toga party in years—I don't even leave the house to do the laundry anymore. I stood there in my bedroom, muttering, "Where . . . ?" They were hiding in the basement, in the dryer. Even more interesting, they were not alone.

I don't have a giant pile of missing clothes in the middle of my basement. But I now own nine unwed socks. The people in my gene pool are more apt to guard against running out of glass jars, lawn tools, bug killer, clay pots . . . (One of my foremothers guarded against running out of Cool Whip containers [sixty-seven], but I was young and sarcastic and didn't own a basement as I stood in hers and counted.) Not too long ago a friend followed me down into my basement, gazed around and then eventually—very politely—she said, "Do you realize that you have six rakes?"

I think it has something to do with the effect of static electricity on the earth's electromagnetic field. Every basement is a black hole for a specific item and dryers are the conduits to a parallel universe, and somewhere in a parallel basement are the six rakes that my friend imagines she saw in mine. These rakes, I suspect, belong to parallel people who are very well-dressed and who store their odd socks in Cool Whip containers.

There is no other explanation.

whitebread

I WAS STILL QUITE YOUNG when I was abducted by Christians—Methodists, by denomination—and forced against my will to go to Sunday school.

Neither of my parents attended church. My father has guided his life for seventy years with a sort of Zen acceptance tinged with a you-can't-do-anything-about-it-anyway fatalism. And, although I'm sure I asked my mother if she believed in God, I don't remember her answer. She did propose the theory that while she might not know what I was up to all of the time, heaven was full of tattletale angels who kept extensive diaries of not only my behavior, but of my thoughts as well. Being her child, I knew exactly whom they reported to. The most religious thing I ever saw my mother DO, however, was write "Protestant" as my religious preference on my school forms. How she arrived at this conclusion is not clear to me, although, after a moment of thought, it is probably as true as the Catholicism or Judaism of some of my adult friends. It is, after all, a cultural value system.

My mother's mother, a proud and devout Protestant, avoided church like the plague, but was driven to tend her religious flame with her passionate disdain for a large, extended family in town she called "the Dagos." I thought it was the family name. The Dagos, she told me, encouraged their children to grow up to be nuns and priests, and the instant this was accomplished, the church changed their children's names and forbade them to ever talk to their parents again. She told me that when she lived in the town where she grew up she lived just down the street from a convent and someone she knew had become a nun, and while she was a novice, this woman was taken for walks by the older nuns and forbidden to even acknowledge her own people who were sitting on the porch watching her walk by. The Catholic Church, in my grandmother's eyes, was anti-family.

My grandmother was not fond of Baptists, either. They were "Holy Rollers," too "full of themselves," and they played with snakes. I understood, even as a child, that Baptists offended my grandmother's sense of decorum—she disapproved of emotional outbursts on principle—but there was probably an ethnic bent to her disapproval that eluded me. I couldn't even tell a Catholic when I saw one, and in the community where I grew up, they were the most obvious minority.

Still, my mother felt some connection to organized religion. When the elderly couple who baby-sat for us offered to take us each week to Sunday school and church, she had us up, dressed appropriately and our stray hairs spit-stuck in place the very next Sunday morning.

We were taken to the Free Methodist Church. I'm not altogether sure what the Free Methodists are "free" of—certainly not rules, regulations or thou-shalt-nots. Dancing, they informed me, was evil. My mother was a square-dance caller. Swearing was evil. Both of my parents, I learned my first day of church, were going to go directly to Hell. I had mixed feelings about this.

I'm not sure how old I was at the time, but it probably wasn't old enough to go anywhere—much less for eternity—without my mom and dad.

For a particular treat, the Free Methodists held a special Sunday night meeting so we could all welcome a returned African missionary. The missionary showed us ninety minutes of slides about disease, pestilence, starvation, unsanitary living conditions and hordes of open, gaping wounds. It was like watching Sally Struthers pitching kids by proxy for $19.95 a month without the humor.

In Sunday school—which we attended faithfully every Sunday before church—we were given lovely religious comic books and the scripture-of-the-week. The comic books had something to do with stories from the Bible, but what I remember most was some ill-tempered pagan goddess named "Kali" who had a penchant for incinerating her followers—or, perhaps that was Pele . . . Kali had four or eight arms and snakes for hair and frequently battled Hercules. I don't remember how all of that related to Bible school. I'm fairly sure the Free Methodists did not intend to intrigue me with tales of pagan goddesses, but I was an odd child even then and you never knew what would stick in my mind.

We held Sunday school under a big picture of a blue-eyed blond man with long hair, wearing a dress and sandals and surrounded by multicolored children. I had never seen multicolored children before. We had to drive all the way to Battle Creek just to see black people. I never questioned that Jesus was a blue-eyed blond. I was a little confused about where all of those Jews came from and why they killed him, thus damning themselves to Hell with my dancing, swearing parents, but my first true, heartfelt quarrel with the Free Methodists had to do with innocence.

The world was full of heathens. I knew this, because the Free Methodists were always raising money to send out missionaries to save the heathens. Heathens were heathens because they worshipped craven gods, or graven images or particularly fat calves. One could be born a heathen, grow up a heathen, be abducted and sent to heathen Sunday school by next-door-neighbor, well-meaning heathens, and eventually die a heathen without ever knowing or ever hearing of the One True God . . . and when you died and met St. Peter at the Pearly Gates, he would send you directly to Hell. Even if you were a good heathen. Even if you brushed your teeth: if you did not know Jesus Christ, if you did not accept Jesus Christ as your savior—even if no one ever introduced you—if you were not SAVED by the Lord . . . do not pass "go," do not collect $200, go directly to Hell. I could accept that people—even my parents—might be told about being saved by Jesus and just stubbornly decide not to anyway, and they might actually . . . sort of, maybe . . . deserve to boil for a while—but I could not see the justice in damning all of those children who were already starving for my vegetables and plagued by pestilence and disease. It seemed to me that a child who actually WANTED to eat canned asparagus deserved a better afterlife.

I hated getting up on Sunday mornings.

I unjoined the Free Methodist Church.

It is the peculiar nature of the way I think that while I, personally, do not believe much of anything I was taught in the Free Methodist Church, I am uncomfortable in most formal religious settings, and "Our Father, who art in heaven. . . ." makes me nervous. I have a distinct and irrational panic reaction to conversations that begin, "I am a Christian and I have been saved . . ." It seems not to ever occur to me that for every Bible-thumping fundamentalist, there may be ten laid-back New Testament Christians who believe Christ was about love and forgiveness and listening to your own inner voice above the noise in the street. I have made my own peace with God, as I perceive God to be. I have accepted Christ—if nothing else—as a far better person than I will ever be.

I have not yet made my peace with church.

second standard

A hundred years
was Sleeping Beauty
sleeping
before Prince Charming
came
and what was the
consolation prize
for waiting
but what the chambermaid
was getting
while Sleeping Beauty
slept.

our house

WHEN I WAS VERY SMALL I lived in the little bedroom next to my parents' room. I approved heartily of the location, but I do not have particularly fond memories of the room itself. For one, it harbored a huge dark green wardrobe I was forbidden to look inside, which therefore hid lions and tigers and hostile elephants. I was prone to nightmares as a child and it was not uncommon for the bears and the tigers to start crawling out of the top of the wardrobe and vault across the room onto my bed and try to maul me in my sleep. I would wake up in hysterics and my mother would come running into the room to find out why I was crying and even when I pointed out the lions she never once saw one.

Even better, the room was papered with a variety of scenes of hostile dwarves, something along the line of Rumplestiltskin, and although it was not a large room, there were probably about a hundred mad dwarves surrounding me. My mother was fond of reading to me and she read any number of stories involving dwarves. Until Snow White came along, I never heard about a friendly dwarf. She would read to me about dwarves who stole babies, dwarves who hid money under the rug, dwarves who cast peculiar spells on people, and then she would kiss me, tuck me in, murmur something encouraging about "bedbugs" and turn out the lights.

I suspect it was the years I lived in this room that explain my serious and residual dislike of *The Wizard of Oz*, which features not only witches, lost children, and lions and tiger and bears— but flying hairy dwarves and several thousand singing chipmunks. I rarely get that far, but I'd rather watch all four versions of *Alien* back-to-back than stick around when those ugly monkeys start coming down out of the sky.

As our family grew it became more and more impractical to keep the babies in bassinets in the dining room, so my room was seized for the common good and I was given a grown-up room upstairs. I had a full-sized bed and room of my own by the age of five. I had arrived. From my bed I could lay and study the light in the hall room, which hung over the stairway back to the rest of my family. At the head of the stairs was a window. Often when the hall light went off, the window at the head of the stairs would be bright with starlight. About a month after I moved upstairs, I spent a weekend with my grandmother, where I sat in rapt attention at her television—we didn't have one—and watched a wonderful story about a man who murdered his wife, skinned her corpse and fashioned her face into a mask which he wore to appear in the window of an older woman's house in order to scare her to death. In fact, he was a ghost story writer and he had previously rented her house. He'd written his best stories there and he wanted her house back. I came home, went to bed, my parents flipped off the stairway light, and I lay frozen in darkness waiting for this ghostly apparition to appear in the hall window between me and any possible escape . . .

The upstairs of our house was a wonderful place to raise children. The stairway came up to a large room we called "the hall" and all of the other rooms opened off from the hall: my room, the little storeroom which had no light and the storeroom beyond that that was full of odd things that smelled funny and *weren't ours* so we couldn't go in there. The spare bedroom, which was closed, was forbidden and hung with dark blinds. Shortly after I left my bedroom downstairs the big, dark green wardrobe that had stored the lions and tigers and bears came upstairs and lived in the corner of the Forbidden Bedroom. My mother stored all of her not-appropriate-for-children books in the wardrobe, including one with a picture of huge extraterrestrial eye that peered down over a city of terrified people who looked very much like our parents.

It was an old house that lived nestled in among a number of big, environmentally friendly trees. A good night in an old, environmentally friendly house is not a quiet night. Squirrels ran up and down the insides of the walls. Boards creaked. Walls groaned. Periodically we were treated to the silent, fluttering sweep of a stray bat. During windstorms the trees would blow in the wind and slap the house upside the head like a truculent child. We named the draft that closed doors when no one was anywhere near them "Simon," but he was nothing compared to the unknown man who lived behind my door and raced me to the light string in the middle of the room each night.

Even deprived of a television, we were able to entertain ourselves in the evening, particularly in the early fall when the migration began. The UnWee and I were sitting on the floor in the living room when some motion whisked past us and our family cat, Gus, charged through the room, froze in the middle of the floor, hunkered down, whiskers twitching, tail-tip flicking right and left, and she c-r-e-p-t, toe-step by toe-step toward the couch . . . We were perhaps eight and five at the time and ever-eager to help, so of course we scrambled on hands and knees across the floor to see what was under the couch. Gus was thoroughly disgusted with us, but the mouse apparently felt outnumbered and made a mad dash for the overstuffed chair. So the mouse dashed, Gus lunged, I vaulted into the seat of the chair to see over the back, my sister ducked under the chair, realized she couldn't see and jumped up for a better look, grazing the bottom of my bare foot with her hair and—I, toe-bitten by a mouse the size of a German shepherd—released a scream that would have frightened the dead. We had a wonderful time explaining what happened to our mother, who seemed to be under the strange impression someone had been maimed or dismembered.

Recently, I have been faulted by a small union of lesser siblings (not all mine) for having failed my role as the hard-core big sister. I have allowed dissension and even outright insubordination from my underlings. It is to these dreamers I devote my last tale of the House of Peck.

In high school the UnWee was the drum major for the Coldwater High School Band. She wore a white sequined bathing suit, white gloves, a big white hat, and white marching boots, and she led the band around the field while threatening them with a baton. They always seemed to go where she sent them. At the end of a particularly grueling day of marching the UnWee clomped onto the back porch in her drum major boots and discovered not a mouse, but a full-grown, living rat. I have never seen a rat in our home and as far as I know the UnWee only saw one, but he was big and he was cocky and he gazed at her with beady little eyes and told her to take a hike. The UnWee did not care for mouse/rat/weasel-like things any more than she enjoys the company of externally-skeletonized or overly-legged things and she quaked in terror at the sight of this rat. The rat, overestimating her fear, thought to himself,

"Hah—another dizzy blond," and he rushed her—or dashed for the door, or moved swiftly and, as it turned out, foolishly . . . The UnWee kicked his soul directly into hell: killed him dead with one blow.

Someone like myself who in her formative youth was terrorized by wallpaper dwarves, doesn't just recklessly lord it over women like the UnWee.

how many lesbians does it take?

I DON'T OWN a cell phone. I have friends who do. They share this information with great pride and enthusiasm, as in (fingers snapping), "You know, we have a cell phone—so we'll turn it on and you can call us at the campgrounds/on the highway/somewhere around the North Pole between 8:10 and 8:15 on the third Tuesday . . ."

I don't know anything about cell phones. They have batteries which are, I gather from my friends' behavior, either extremely short-lived, or more precious than life itself. I had a doll who wore a white bridal dress and because her dress was white I could never play with her because she would get "dirty." That experience satisfied my need to own something that never does anything. So I have no idea why anyone would want a cell phone. Certainly I don't need one: I have a portable phone that hangs up on me on whim so I have battery concerns enough of my own.

So I was phoneless (uncelled?) when I invited friends (2) to come spend an evening with us at my Beloved's house, and I mentioned casually that one of them had enjoyed, once, a year or so ago, the company of a friend we have in common. In slightly over a week this became a ten-person steak picnic in the park with fresh strawberries ladled over homemade cheesecake, designated grill tenders and a trail of lost dinner guests. I—who would probably not carry a peanut butter sandwich outside to eat in a lawn chair because it's too much work—watched this whole process with mild amazement. I had a good vantage point to watch this because the grill, the eleven lawn chairs, the potato casserole, three coolers and a fishing pole crawled up in the back of my truck and waited impatiently for transport.

There were women standing on the riverbank sharing fly-fishing techniques. There were flocks of geese eyeing the coolers. There were big, graceful willows snapping greedily at the lines of the fly-fishing women. There were mallards flying in, landing on their breasts and making a sweet waterfall sound as they glided to a stop. In the background the peacocks in the little zoo across the river were crying like lost children in the woods.

The food was plentiful and delicious, the company was happy and relaxed, the heat, which was oppressive, was more bearable in the presence of friends, and the steaks were grilled to taste and perfection. It was a thoroughly delightful evening until, seconds from the end, our Friend In Common, Alice, stuck her key in the ignition of her car and thought:

That's not my key.

And she was absolutely right. It was not her key. It was the key of a friend. She had accepted the task of daycare provider for a friend's Ford and she had stuck her friend's key in her own ignition. The car would not start. The correct key would not go into the ignition, having been so recently dispossessed, and neither key would start the car. The key said to Alice—*foo to you, you ingrate, I resign.*

The car, barely a year old and not even yet scratched, would not start.

I drive a scratched, dented, fender-bent, four-year-old truck

I've named "Hoppy," which has enough keys to start a dealership. (Hoppy, being a GM, takes two keys just to make him go—he came with four and the warranty will provide a spare each time I lock myself out for the first 75,000 miles. By now there is a spare door key for Hoppy under every rock and bush between Jackson and Three Rivers.) None of my keys, however, are "coded." I have no little plastic box with buttons to push to make the car start.

Being intelligent, car-savvy lesbians, we determined that the daycare key had fouled up the recognition mechanism in the ignition. The key had been decoded. Alice had been foiled by her own anti-theft devices.

And because Alice is quirky about her vehicles and guards them with her life—possibly even with her partner's life, should it ever come to that—it looked very much as if Alice and her partner were going to have to set up camp among the geese in the park.

Fortunately, my Beloved could provide virtually everything they might need for the night. They could feed themselves easily into late Tuesday evening. They had chairs, a grill, a fly rod, several nice flies, a river . . . All the duck and goose anyone could care to eat . . . I was ready to go home.

Someone said, "Hey—I have a cell phone."

I don't know who that person was. She was never seen nor heard from again. There in the middle of a parking lot at 10:30 at night stood ten sweating lesbians, a dead Ford, thirty-seven still-hopeful geese and a cell phone no one knew how to operate. It was as if the phone fairy had dropped the Rubik's Cube of communications in our hands and then dusted away all of our memories of her.

Thea, Eliza and Alice's partner, Rhonda, all own cell phones, but this particular cell phone was alien to all of them. Eliza was busy waving magnets at the ignition. Alice—who owned the car—was distracted because Lucylou was thinking about dismantling something under the hood with a flashlight and an ice pick. I know nothing about cell phones but I can see: Thea knows a great deal about cell phones, but is legally blind without stadium lights. Lucylou was digging through her tool box for a plumber's wrench, which was troublesome because Alice was the only one who knew the help number we were calling and we could not seem to keep her attention away from Lucylou's banging long enough to get it dialed. So while Lucylou was humming to herself and banging blunt metal objects against the car engine, Thea would activate the phone, hand it to me, I would dial 800 and then shout and scream until Alice looked up at me with a distracted, almost panicked look in her eye and murmured something about closing the hood, the cell phone would die, and we would start the whole process all over again.

It began to occur to us that we had become a living joke—how many lesbians does it take to operate a cell phone?

The answer appears to be ten. One to turn it on, one to dial the number, one to recite the number to be dialed, one to bang on the engine with a plumber's wrench, one to fly fish, two to chase the geese away, one to hold the flashlight, one to unload the trunk, and one to jimmy the key in the lock, repeating, "This really should work. . . ."

We did rescue Alice. Kind of. Sort of. We told the panic line, with great assurance, that the key had not broken off in the lock, it was an ignition problem, so rather than a locksmith they sent a wrecker guy, who promptly noted the key had broken off in the lock. He did not have the tools to fix it.

So my Beloved lent Alice her car, and we took everything out of our friend's trunk and put it in my Beloved's trunk, just as the wrecker man said, "You know, I should be able to get that."

So we got everything back out of my Beloved's trunk and put it back in Alice's trunk, just as the wrecker man said, "No, I guess not . . ."

So we got everything out of our friend's trunk and we put it in my Beloved's trunk.

Alice is going to have to leave Rhonda and my Beloved is going to have to leave me because their stuff is so commingled after about the sixth trunk swap they will never be able to live independently again.

But we got everyone home, out of the park, and I don't believe we even hit any geese.

I still don't own a cell phone, but I may take the plumber's wrench out of my truck for safety's sake. You can never be sure which one of your friends will be most willing to bang on your engine. However helpful that might be.

my mother's eyes

This morning your face
was in my mirror: the same
yellow/green eyes, the same
odd cindered flecks, the same
laughlines at the corners, the same
age.
You are frozen in time.
Preserved, like my plaster
kindergarten handprints, or
snap shot and printed as
a gap-toothed six-year-old
beaming proudly at the helm
of her brand-new bike.
My father, aging gracefully,
stands on the cusp of becoming
an older man, but you—who hated
aging—are forever forty-nine.
For twenty-two years you have
stayed the same, no after-images
to betray you, while I look in my mirror

and I see your face
your eyes.
In seven days
I will be older
than any image I have
of you.

frogs

IT IS A BEAUTIFUL DAY, nearly 70 degrees outside before the sun even awoke. Spring is stirring. The sap is running. Tiny, half-formed ideas of life are beginning to poke up out of the ground. Three evenings ago I drove past a wetland and I heard a sound I have not heard in years—the chorus of wide-awake and amorous frogs advertising their wares: *For a good time check out lily pad number 614. Distinguished gentleman in emerald greatcoat paging spotted lady with long legs. No reasonable offer refused.* The chorus of frog ponds. I know a great deal about frogs.

I can remember when we believed perhaps a little less that the world should conform to our expectations, and it was the responsibility of the driver to maneuver the road and not of the road to stay under the driver. The road that ran in front of our house—Battle Creek Road then, Union City Road now, a country road that has changed its name to acknowledge a small (but very picturesque) wide spot not even square in the middle of it—crossed a free-flowing wetland just north of my parents' yard. The wetland on the right of the highway was connected to the wetland on the left of the highway by a culvert that ran under the road, and, based on my scientific observations as a child, all of the boy frogs were born on the right and all of the girl frogs were born on the left. When spring came and the sap began to run, all of the frogs from both wetlands met in the middle of the road to begin their courtship. It was not an exceptionally busy highway, but there is never much mystery about the outcome of a collision between a frog and a car, and over a period of about six days and nights when frogs apparently act out all of their sexual urges for the entire year, the highway would develop a distinct frog coating. There were dead frogs everywhere. The dip between the highlands and the lowlands on that particular stretch of road was sudden and rather startling to the uninitiated—and particularly so to the drunk—and the smooth patina of deceased frogs did nothing to improve traction or handling. And so it came to pass that some unfortunate soul, weaving his way home from a bar, parked his car rather unexpectedly in the swamp. I would not have parked my car there. The men who came to operate the three wreckers, the bulldozer and the crane that came to pluck him out all agreed they would not have parked their cars there, but in those days one did not get much sympathy for being the victim of a frog attack. Particularly when the frogs were dead.

The Road Commission came out shortly after that and built the road up until there was no appreciable dip. Perhaps they were annoyed because the drunk lived. The highway became something of a climb for a sex-starved frog and over time there came to be fewer and fewer frogs in the gravel pit. Some have blamed this on changes in the climate and acid rain, but I blame the Road Commission and a little-known natural phenomena known as "recruitment." I would think that by the time one has tried to climb Mount Everest just for a hot date, fellow boy frogs—or sister girl frogs—who are distinctly more convenient, may just look a whole lot better. It is possible the entire frog pond community just turned gay and died out.

There are other factors leading to the disappearance of the common frog that I feel have been underestimated by the scientific community, not the least of which is basic intelligence. A friend of mine who is six feet two inches and certainly not a fragile thing recently told me a tale about going to a Mexican restaurant with friends and feeling uneasy about speaking frankly about his lifestyle (which does not even include eating flies with his tongue). When I failed to appreciate his dilemma, he reminded me of the possibility of meeting a herd of young men waving two-by-fours. My friend has well-honed survival instincts. And it curiously brought me back to remembering the last frog I saw. Was he soaking up the sun's rays through two or three feet of mud? Was he sitting on a lily pad in the middle of the lake? No, the last one I saw was hopping for his life down the bank, a herd of small boys waving sticks and shrieking with the glee of the hunt behind him.

A year or so ago I was driving down the road, minding my own business, when a frog leaped into my headlights and disappeared under the wheels of my truck. I believe I have already mentioned that given not one but two entire wetlands in which to conduct their personal business, the vast majority of frogs were driven to display their every intimate moment on a slab of asphalt twelve feet wide and perhaps an eighth of a mile long. I believe suicide is a seriously understudied social problem for frogs. I believe the most that can be said for frogs is that they have a curious inability to see and identify an obvious natural enemy.

Which leads me to the subject of lawn mowers. My father the groundskeeper woke every summer morning to wander out into his yard and measure each blade of grass that grew there and the second one blade grew any taller than any of the others, he would say, "Cheryl—have you looked at the lawn?"

Being more a chattel really than a groundskeeper I could only remark that it seemed quite green to me.

"Needs to be mowed," he would announce, and then he would go off to work.

I hated mowing the lawn as a child. I hated work as a child: but I hated mowing the lawn for two reasons. The mower. And frogs. The mower would never start for me. I could spend hours yanking the string, to have it cough, choke, splutter and die. I could kick it, swear at it, throw small stones at it, threaten it, yank the rope again . . . the mower would never start. If it did start, it would die two rows later and never start again. My father would come home. He would get out of his car. He would stretch. He would look around. He would purse his lips. He would say, "What happened to the lawn, Cheryl?"

I would answer, "The mower won't start."

He would say, "Did you put gas in it?"

I would always swear I had, although, in truth, that particular task would never occur to me because it was my father's mower and my father never kept a tool without all of its required fluids in his life. I did not have any concept of how many fluids male tools need until some time after I left my father's house when, one by one, all of my tools ran dry.

He would look annoyed, possibly because he had five children and two jobs and his oldest child was not even bright enough to run a lawn mower, and we would walk over to the offending mower, and he would look at it, check the gas, check some other fluid, walk all the way around it twice, and then reach out and pull the string and POOF!

The mower started.

I watched this ritual perhaps two hundred times before it finally dawned on me that lawn mowers are afraid of circles, much preferring straight lines, and they will do anything to keep you from walking around them that third time—even start, if need be.

So, having spent the entire day not mowing the lawn, I would

frogs

now have my entire evening tied up in grass and I would trudge glumly along behind the mower, mowing frogs.

Frogs are curiously attracted to lawn mowers. They are apparently more hypnotic than car headlights are for deer. Perhaps it is the noise. Frogs will come from miles around to hop into the spinning blades of a lawn mower and be fileted, pureed and sprayed like fine pink mist all over the shins of slave labor. For the record, frog bones hurt.

As I drove this spring past the wetland where the frogs were singing mating calls to the frogs on the other side of the road, I was touched for a moment with nostalgia. What a delightful, primordial sound. It was almost like being home again, listening to the pop pop pop of those little frog bodies in the road.

mother/spirit

Sometimes
I can feel your will
lean in behind me,
your breath hot
on my cheek
as you whisper words
I can no longer hear.
The silence doesn't matter.
Threatening/reassuring,
you always meant:
Remember me—
    I'm right here.

batting a thousand

I WAS SITTING at the keyboard and Babycakes was sitting on my shoulder, half-asleep (both the cat and the shoulder) when an utterly silent shadow rippled across the room.

I thought, *There's a bird in this room.*

Something was amiss, I could tell by the repetitive lashing of my left ear by the cat's tail.

A *large bird*, I reflected, reviewing my memory, *black and swooping—probably a rogue turkey vulture.*

But I sat at my keyboard and the cat sat on my shoulder, and for the longest time nothing happened.

It's all your imagination, I reproved myself. *Perhaps it was merely a giant moth.*

And at that exact moment, an utterly silent shadow swooped across the room.

The cat bolted off my shoulder, taking along small bits of my skin, and huddled down on the floor where he made himself into a small gold rug with big accusing gold eyes, which he trained on me, as if to say, *What have you done now?*

Circling my light like a drunken glider was a bat.

I know very little about bats now and I knew even less then.

This bat was small and brown. (This observation is unusually precise. Experts in batology would have called it a small brown bat. I did not know this, at the time.)

When I stood up, the circle the bat was flying around my light became more elliptical, as if something large and horrifying had wandered into its radar. I looked around, but I never did see what it was.

I spoke to the bat. I said, "Go away."

I walked over to the window, raised the screen, and posed, not altogether unlike Vanna White. "Here would be a good place to go," I directed.

The bat switched the tilt of his ellipse from one side of the room to the other. Beyond that I could see no real change in his behavior. He swept past me once, dangerously close to my hair, which I interpreted as an act of aggression.

I may have shrieked.

(Once. It was one of those girl-instinct things that sometimes gets the better of me.)

I went back to the other side of the room, beside the keyboard, and waited.

The bat stopped circling. He had thrown up some subsonic invisibility ray to disguise his whereabouts.

I looked expectantly at the cat.

The cat looked disgusted and bathed a wild hair.

I thought to myself, *leave the screen open, close the computer room door and go to bed—when you wake up in the morning, the bat will be gone.*

Or, thirty thousand of his closest friends will be partying in the computer room. There will be stale beer and corn nuts all over the keyboard, small drunken aviators will be hanging upside down from the curtain rods . . .

Bats are good, my conscience lectured me, *don't do anything to hurt this innocent little bat.*

So I closed the screen, closed the door and snuck myself and the cat out of the computer room and went to bed.

In the morning the bat did seem to have vacated the premises.

The following night I was sitting at the keyboard with a sleeping cat on my sleeping shoulder when an utterly silent shadow rippled across the room.

The cat lunged off my shoulder, taking most of my right arm with him, and hid under the desk.

"That's it," I said, "I'm done—get out of my house."

And I went for the tennis racket.

(We will take a moment from our narrative to allow all of my personal friends to finish turning to one another and murmuring, "Cheryl Peck owns a tennis racket?" I do. I stole it from the Wee One because I could see no reason why my little sister should own a tennis racket when I didn't. I don't play tennis, but then again, I might. Besides, she quit playing right after that.)

My plan was simple, but well organized: I would swing the tennis racket, knocking the bat out of the air into a small trash can I held in the other hand. I would then slam the tennis racket over the top of the can, constructing a makeshift jail long enough to carry my prisoner downstairs and outside to freedom, where he would gratefully fly away.

The cat at my heels was just insurance. Somewhat wimpy insurance, judging from the cowering crouch, but I assured myself that once the bat had stopped, it would look to the cat like what it looked to me—a flying mouse. The cat has never been out of the house and mice have never been in the house, but I trusted fervently that instincts would burst into play at the appropriate moment.

I swung my tennis racket. I caught a solid draft of sheer air, nearly knocking myself off balance, while the bat circled around and swooped just over my head.

I waited, muscles tensed for action, instincts honed, my heart pounding with the lust to kill: I swung again, nearly decapitated the cat, drove my own knee forcefully into the trash can as I stumbled forward, and I cursed myself for every tennis lesson I never took.

On the third swing I knocked the bat out of the air onto the ground, where it twitched twice, attached itself to the grid of my tennis racket and began crawling up the handle. Swiftly, possibly shrieking (for only the second time in my life), I scraped the offending creature into the trash can, where it hung upside down, still glued to the racket. All three of us thundered down the stairs to the front door where a passionate discussion ensued concerning who can go outside and who cannot. In the meantime, the bat was shaking his battered little head and beginning to stir. The cat would not give up: he would go outside and oversee the release of the bat, or no one would go outside. He glued his back to the door, his paws spread, nailed against the door like a tiny hairy Jesus figure.

I explained that if he had been a proper cat, he would have caught the bat, eaten it and I would never have had to deal with the situation at all.

He spoke to me about the lure of the wild life, the faint perfume of wanton females in the wind, the sheer testosterone of hunting and killing his own food.

I set the trash can on the floor, its inmate twitching erratically against its mesh caging.

"Okay, so perhaps not," huffed the cat. He flicked his tail at me and stalked with great dignity into the kitchen.

I carried the bat outside and released him.

Or, at least I tried.

I waved him toward freedom.

The bat remained glued to the tennis racket.

I waited for the scent of freedom to call him.

He wrapped his wings around his head and pretended to be dead.

To the bat I said, "Give me back my tennis racket." For, having used this racket to play one game of tennis in the thirteen years it had hung in my basement stairway, I was loath to leave it outside, unattended, in the wind and the weather to warp and perhaps be destroyed.

"Get off, get off," I wailed, and began dancing the hopping, puppering whines of the terminally mature.

The cat poked his head through the curtains to see what I was up to, and then went away.

I scraped the bat off my tennis racket against the stone flower box on my front porch not unlike the way one would remove peanut butter from a knife blade.

"Die there, then," I tossed as my parting shot.

The bat, batted and bewildered, cat-threatened and smashed and trashed—and, very likely, hungry—gathered his tiny bat wings up, shook them off, staggered a few steps down the flower box, then gathered himself together and flew unsteadily off into the sunset.

I suspect he warned his friends.

Fear the mighty dyke that lives in that house, he told them all. *That woman has a shriek that will foul up your radar for days.*

the chicken coupe

I DO LOVE PRESENTS and there is a special place in my heart for Christmas, but as a child my favorite—all-time, hands-down *favorite*—holiday was Easter. When we were very young all three of us girls were made brand-new Easter dresses, a tradition that dwindled down gradually as it became clear we never went anywhere to wear them, and even clearer that—except for that doll-loving sissy, the Wee One—none of us even liked dresses all that much. However, the new dresses took care of that perpetual gift-giving foolery, clothes. I was never deeply enamored of the idea of getting clothes as a gift. A "gift," to me, was something wonderful and exciting and new and especially mine. It seemed a given, to me, even at an early age, that one way or another we would get clothes: to wrap them up in pretty paper and put a ribbon on them seemed to me to be cheating. But by Easter we had already gotten the clothes, so there was not much danger of rushing downstairs in the morning and finding our baskets full of underwear or more frilly little dresses to wear to school.

No, our baskets would be full of candy.

Chocolate.

I loved chocolate.

There may never have been a child born who loved chocolate more than I did.

Every Easter, in my basket—dead center in my basket—would be a big, molded something made of pure milk chocolate.

Solid chocolate.

Rabbits made of chocolate, most often.

The Easter I was six, the molded milk chocolate in my basket was a chicken.

I was ecstatic. It was a very large chicken, by small child standards, and therefore it was a great deal of chocolate. It looked so good I began drooling the moment I saw it. I was overwhelmed by chocolate lust.

Even as an adult I do not have a great deal of restraint when it comes to chocolate. Delayed gratification has never been a strong goal for me. As a child I had almost no restraint. Every year my mother gave me a huge basket full of Easter candy, and every year my mother took it away from me again at least by noon because I saw no reason to have a huge basket full of Easter candy unless I could sit right down on the floor and eat the whole thing. I do not have a "full" button that lights up and tells me to quit eating. I do not have an "enough" button that ever lights up for anything. As a child or an adult, I can literally eat until whatever I am eating is gone. I may be uncomfortable later, but at the time there is nothing to warn me of the coming consequences.

As a child I could not bring myself to believe there could be any bad consequences from eating anything so good as chocolate.

I was, however, extraordinarily proud of my chocolate chicken, and I said to my mother, "I'm going to take this over and show it to my Gramma Peck."

I had a mission.

It was a mission with a flaw, but a mission nonetheless.

So I did not eat my chicken while we were all piling into

the car, because I was taking it to my Gramma Peck to show it to her.

I did not eat my chicken during the six miles around Randall Lake, around Swan's Curve, or through the farmlands before and after Hodunk. We turned on Stancer Road and I did not eat my chicken as we passed the millpond and drove by the Electric City Mill.

But somewhere between the Electric City Mill and the corner of Stancer and Adolf Roads someone bit the head off my chicken.

I was horrified.

All that work, all that restraint, all that suffering and self-control . . . all for nothing.

I had nothing to show my grandmother but a headless chicken.

A chicken decapitated by my own greed.

I began sobbing hysterically.

"What on earth is wrong with you?" my mother checked from the front seat.

Holding up the evidence of my moral failure, I sobbed, "I bit the head off my chicken."

There are those cherished moments in life when parents are reminded of the simple truths of childhood. This was apparently not one of those moments. "Oh, for Chrissake," my mother said supportively and turned back to face the front.

So sobbing, huge tears running off my cheeks, I clamored into my grandmother's house, held up my headless chicken, and confessed, "IwantedtoshowyoumychickenbutIatetheheadoff (*hic*) . . ."

My grandmother said, "Was it good?"

And indeed it was.

maiden voyage

THE SUMMER I MET my Beloved, she took a month off from life and went to Alaska, where she and two friends paddled kayaks around Prince William Sound.

The summer I met my Beloved, I took a day off work alleging I was ill and sat on the couch eating junk food and watching '70s cop-show reruns on TV.

We have never been a perfect match.

The following summer my Beloved bought a kayak and a 20-speed mountain bike. Every day I would talk to her on the phone and every day she would tell me where she rode that morning before work. Every day I would share with her that I dragged myself out of bed and into the shower, threw on some clothes and once again made it to work without actually, technically being late. It occurred to me, sometime during that second summer, that my Beloved wakes up, ready to move and talk and function—nearly ready to sing—in the wee wee hours of the morn. Before the worms have had their chance to turn. Before the early birds have begun thinking about their breakfast. And she would then don her biking gear and take off for adventure and discovery and . . . pleasure.

This led, of course, to our first fight, which had something to do with distance. She told me one morning that she had ridden about five miles that day to a particular dam and back. Now, according to the odometer on my truck, when I reached that dam I was twelve miles from her house. One way. This lent new and dark meanings to such enticements as, "Oh, come on—we'll just go for a short ride." In my biking prime, practicing faithfully, going to the gym religiously, I had worked myself into such a state of fitness that I could ride my bike twenty-five miles in one day before turning scarlet, wilting like old lettuce and needing three to six hours of sleep. This meant, of course, that a "short" ride with my Beloved was a mere 35–50 miles round-trip. A mere teasing of the biking muscles. A "warmup," as my sports physiologist/sadist/torturist might say.

I recalled for my Beloved my favorite bike ride—it may have been the last—which took place in mid-September, during the blooming of some unseen and undiagnosed allergen, which sucks the oxygen from my asthma and leaves me huffing and puffing in the dust. They SAID the ride was 25 miles. I carry an odometer on my bike for just such misrepresentations. I rode along with a friend for 25 miles, stopping to gasp and wheeze and apologize every mile or so, until at one point we abandoned our bikes on the edge of a particularly scenic hay field and planned my funeral. We rode 25.5 miles. We rode 25.75 miles. One of our beginning-of-the-ride companions drove past to encourage us and tell us breezily that the ride had bored her so she had taken the 40-mile route. I mentioned that—according to my bike—I had already gone 25 miles—which was all I had signed up for—and the finish line was not visible to my naked eyes.

"Oh, no, it's about five miles up," our friend said cheerfully, "and that last two miles is a killer—wind, you know . . ."

I said, "So I have already ridden twenty-five miles, and they lied about the length."

"Oh, yeah," she said blithely.

I slammed that bike on the carrier on the back of her Jeep and jumped into the front seat.

"I guess she's done," Blithe Spirit observed.

I grew up on the water. The song of a red-winged blackbird calls home to me. I dislike canoes because they're tipsy and with my compromised sense of balance they lack that feeling of security that the living room couch provides, but kayaks are lower in the water. You can actually touch the water, which has long been a bitter complaint I've held against other boats. Were you floating leisurely down a river in a kayak and were you attacked by a tree, you could reach up and push the offending foliage aside without guaranteeing you and your partner would be touching the water within the second.* And in kayaks there is no "partner." No one behind you in the boat, shifting and bobbling about, shouting orders about the "other paddle" or "your other right."

For a long time I allowed friends to convince me canoeing down the Pere Marquette River near Baldwin was fun. I became something of a legend for my skill and prowess in a canoe. My friend Bob admiringly admitted he has never heard anyone shriek so loudly or so long over so little. He has told many a fond tale of our adventures, and he has assured me with great affection that we will remain friends forever as long as I never crawl into his canoe again. Not that Bob is in any great danger of sneak attacks.

*Do not try this at home.

I write to be amusing. However, for the water-impaired: the number one rule in moving watercraft, whether it is an inner tube or a cigarette boat is never, never, NEVER grab any stationary object while in a moving water vehicle. Never. If you have any doubts, get in the front of Bob's canoe and listen to his minute-by-minute instructions down the river. It will be quite clear by the time you reach shore again.

Even clearer if you've gotten him wet.

In the interest of togetherness, sharing and mutual water love this spring I bought my own kayak. My Beloved and I took it home. Stored it in my Beloved's shed next to hers. From time to time we would go out and admire it. Never one to rest when there is more to be done, my Beloved insisted we actually take them out in the water.

So I launched my new boat.

I put my right foot in.

I took my right foot out.

I put my right foot in and I waffled all about . . .

While my Beloved kayaked up and down the shoreline offering encouragement and loving threats of death and dismemberment, I contemplated my body, which is large and awkward and stiff and slow-moving, and those various qualities of water I have long loved . . . it's fast, it's slippery, it's wet . . .

In a mere thirty-five minutes I had tucked my ample behind into my kayak and was paddling in firm circles around the pond.

After a little more direction and encouragement from my Beloved I began pursuing straight lines across the pond—and we were off.

The Hoffman Pond, which we had chosen for our maiden voyage, is, in many places, about a foot deep. It is gently lined with lily pads and staunchly guarded by a small flock of killer swans and a hundred or so Canada geese. I was paddling peacefully through the lily pads, doing my best to avoid the swans, when the bottom of the pond exploded against my hull and nearly plunged me into the drink.

Ever alert to my most subtle mood, my Beloved called, "What are you screaming about now?"

"The pond is exploding," I reported. "Part of it just came up and slapped my ass."

"Carp," she said.

A few paddles farther upstream it happened again. Carp—

those exaggerated colorless goldfish that grow to be the size of small whales—were busy with the business of spring under the lily pads and whenever I floated over one (or two), it would lunge and flop and bang against the underside of the boat. I am not entirely certain how carp do manage the business of spring and I was hoping fervently that they were not trying to do to my boat what they were doing to each other under the lily pads. Nor, apparently, can one count on the common sense of a carp to avoid future collisions. I swear one struggled out from under my bow and slammed headfirst into the stern.

Still, it was a beautiful, calm evening on the pond. Swans eyed us beadily, but had not yet swept their wings out for a full attack. The water birds sang, a very faint breeze licked coolly against our skin, the sun was beginning to set . . .

I had found the perfect sport.

I loved kayaking.

I could kayak all day.

Ahead of me my Beloved shifted restlessly in her own boat. "So, Cheryl," she called back, "were you thinking of starting to paddle anytime soon . . . ?"

clean sheets

You're back, I see.
It's been awhile.
I heard you'd been living
with some woman
further south—
not the one you dumped
for me, or the one you dumped
me for, or the one you left
both of us to have—
a new one.
One I never met.
You do love your
clean sheets.

a cover story

MY SISTER (the UnWee) and I slept upstairs. We were the only ones. Every night we kissed our mom and dad goodnight (giving up all hope of ever seeing them alive again) and climbed up those dark, creaking stairs into our dark, creaking rooms—hers in the hall, mine even deeper into the attic than that—leapt over the child-eating monsters that snaked out from under our beds, burrowed down into our covers and waited as our parents—the wardens—turned off the lights. We were imprisoned in darkness for the night.

I was terrified of the dark.

I was afraid of the shapeless, scurrying things that ran up and down the walls of our old farmhouse, and I was afraid of the huge, way-too-close things that banged against the walls outside, and I was afraid of the dark, silent swooshing things that flew through the air after the lights went out (*"There's a bat in here!"*), but I reserved my deepest and screamless terror for two things: The Man Who Lived Behind My Bedroom Door, and The Book.

The UnWee remembers The Book. She slept even closer to it than I did.

The irony of all this is that we couldn't just tell our mother we couldn't sleep upstairs because of The Book because we weren't supposed to know it was there.

We'd snooped.

We were bad once (okay, so we were bad twice, or maybe three times or four or five—RELATIVELY we were innocents) and our punishment was years of nights, night after night, of lying there, in the dark, waiting. We knew The Book was there.

Sooner or later, it would get us.

Our mother loved to read and our house was full of books. Not rows of matching leather-bound tomes filed in stately wooden shelves—our mother read paperbacks and she kept her library in grocery sacks. She apparently knew other people who read as well, because every now and then women would come to our house and there would be this mad, exciting exchange— not of individual volumes—but of BAGS of volumes. Agatha Christie, Mickey Spillane, Victoria Holt (she must be 110 by now), Henry Miller and . . . I can't think of his name—he wrote at least twenty books about rich people who dabbled in politics and (ate carrots) like bunnies (ah, yes—Harold Robbins) . . . romance novels, spy novels, detective novels . . . They all had one theme in common—sex—which I discovered quite early in my reading career (being naturally curious about such things) and I spent any number of secret hours during my teen years looking for the books my mother had determined were not fit for me to read. She read voraciously and she acquired so many bags of books that she had to find places to put them until the next group of book-starved women came along.

There is a peculiar inherited gene in our family that (apparently) lies dormant until the women conceive and then vaults like Tipper Gore out of a Morally Upright birthday cake and drives them to Make the World Safe for Children. My mother read *Tropic of Capricorn* while the local women's club was drawing up a petition to have Henry Miller drawn and quartered in the adult reading room of the public library—but let MY virgin little fingers touch that book and you would have sworn seven HIV-positive transvestites had just tried to shake hands with Jesse Helms. It was this gene that caused my mother to sort her books into two piles: those suitable for small children to peruse and those that would corrupt our mortal souls.

(Did I mention that my younger sister and I were the only two people in the family to sleep upstairs?)

This same gene caused my mother—normally a sane woman—to pack up all of these corrupt, unclean, filthy, sexually explicit X-rated seducers of the Innocent Youth of America and store them

**upstairs
in the storeroom
and say, "Don't come in here."**

This mysterious, unknown storeroom full of . . . things . . . that we had never seen before, belonging to—who knew?—and barred from our curious explorations by . . . a doorknob. And an order. "STAY OUT."

And it was effective. Our mother would get into the car to drive a mile down the road to the store and the UnWee and I would race up the stairway and burst into the storeroom to explore.

The storeroom was dark, sealed into eternal gloom by the heavy dark green shades that were drawn over the windows all of the time. It had a kind of musty, abandoned smell. I remember there was a dresser and in one of the drawers of the dresser was a tube of scarlet lipstick that somehow escaped, smeared all over our clothes and got us into a peck of trouble. In the corner, all but hiding behind the door like The Man Behind the Door in my own room, was this H-U-G-E dark green two-doored wooden storage-thing that held (among other things) my grandfather's Knights Templar uniform, which was mysterious enough for a seven-year-old. And in this darkened room, behind the door, in this huge green closet-thing, in a grocery bag—on top of the grocery bag—was The Book.

They don't make books like The Book anymore. It was a '50s thing. A crowd of terrified men and women (all in suits and ties/dresses and heels) ran in all directions from this huge EYE that peered down at them from the sky.

We took one look at that horrid thing and we knew we were doomed.

We weren't supposed to be in the green thing.

We weren't supposed to be in the storeroom.

We didn't even know what that eye-thing was, but it saw us, and it knew where we had been, and we knew in our hearts that the next time it got dark that eye-thing was going to crawl out of that bag, out of the green thing, out of the storeroom altogether and come after us and it was going to do . . . whatever inexplicable thing it was already doing to all of those terrified, overdressed adults.

If memory serves me correctly—and it doesn't, always—I believe I actually summoned the courage to read The Book when I was older. It may have been titled *The Day the World Ended* and it may have been a fairly insipid sci-fi tale about how the earth narrowly avoided being eliminated by some extraterrestrial terrorist organization when Our Scientist sneezed and then sprayed them with salt water . . . or maybe not. I think I remember that it was an incredibly bland story for such a horror-inspiring cover, that I had spent years cowering from some inner fear I could not begin to articulate and after I read the book, I just felt silly.

When the Wee One moved upstairs she was lodged in the hall and the storeroom was cleaned out and it became the Un-Wee's room. I never saw The Book again. I can't prove this, but I think she said to herself, "I'm not living in this room with The Book." And she killed it.

thinking of you

He will jump up
and settle into my lap,
a low purr in his throat,
the occasional nail-stretch
gripping me
as he gazes, eyes half-closed,
across the room.
His whole body will arch
under my hand, absorbing
contact while he hums,
muscle and throat,
and for each stroke
he presses harder
until we are nearly
one.

Touch me, you said,
the way you touch
your cat.

truer confessions

I HAVE ALWAYS PRESENTED my childhood as if it were nearly idyllic, five happy siblings gamboling hand-in-hand across waving fields of grain with nothing on their minds more serious than a herd of homicidal cows. The truth is much darker and more difficult to face. I was horribly abused as a child. I was forced to wash dishes.

Every day.

Whether I wanted to or not.

I have friends who have been irrevocably scarred by experiences like mine, friends with their original character broken, their brains washed and filled with foolish adult mantras such as task assigned/task completed. I alone stood up solidly against this kind of brutal conditioning. My hands are soapy, but unbowed.

I held fast to the belief that my mom could tell me what to do, but there was always the chance that I could drive her to that final moment of surrender when she would swear under her breath and mutter, *it's just easier to do it myself*.

We all develop our own survival skills. Mine was dragging out a task into slow, torturous frame-by-frame motion that seemed to take forever. It could take me as long as four and a half hours to wash supper dishes for seven people. My father used to wander out into the kitchen and just stand in the doorway, scowling at me, as if he were utterly baffled. A task assigned/task completed veteran, it was inconceivable to him that anyone could drag out a simple task that long—or would even want to.

My mother would say cold, manipulative things like, "You know, Sherry, if you would just buckle down and GET IT DONE, you'd have time to do the things you want to do."

By most accounts—certainly by any you might hear from my siblings—I was an odd child. I spent most of my childhood wandering around in the gravel pit behind our house where I made up stories in my head about my imaginary friends. I certainly preferred this to reality, a perception which seemed to pester my mother to no end. I spent so much time in the company of those who were not there—and so much of it walking—that I wore regular paths all through the gravel pit where I walked and retraced my steps, back and forth and back and forth again. My only living companion was a black cat, Bugles, who perfected the art of weaving back and forth between my feet so that we walked in perfect synchronization, sometimes for hours.

By my account, the only form of amusement that ever seemed to present itself to my lesser siblings was to sneak down into the gravel pit and hide behind rocks and giggle when I walked by. Sometimes they would push a young one out of hiding and the child would look at me goggle-eyed, then scowl suspiciously and demand, "Who are you talking to?"

I did not simply walk. Particularly dramatic moments might make me leap forward or break into a short run. I waved and gesticulated. I was a gunfighter, a swordswoman, or the fearless captain of some rocking, storm-tossed galleon. My imagination was a cross between mental movie making and a one-person theater, so that I spoke aloud—or at least whispered—my particularly moving lines. I suppose it is remotely possible that someone merely looking on, without any real appreciation for the creative process, might, in a nonsupportive moment, have labeled such a performance "crazy."

Not that any of my siblings did so to my face. For one, I was bigger than they were. Our parents occasionally left us alone and then they were at my mercy. I rarely beat them up and I sometimes even remembered to feed them, but I have no recollection of being a particularly warm or friendly big sister and it was probably clear to them that I liked them best when they were somewhere else. From time to time the Wee One would materialize through the mist that I preferred to have surrounding me and she would frown solemnly, in her much-younger way, and say, "Cheryl . . . you know when you're walking around down in the gravel pit . . . who are you talking to?" As if there were a simple, logical answer to that question.

As it happened, my tradition of taking long walks with invisible friends worked in quite well with my dishwashing routine. All water in our house drained into a somewhat temperamental septic system, so we were barely allowed to dump the dirty dishwater down the drain, much less scraps of food or peelings or skins. So each evening I would fill my dish tub with hot, soapy water, soak the glasses and carry a plate to the back of our yard where we threw our garbage over the bank. I scraped the plates one plate at a time. If a particularly dramatic storyline unfolded itself mid-scrape, I might walk the same plate back and forth several times while I played with the threads of my plots, or unknotted a particularly tangled characterization.

I did this less often in the winter than the summer for two reasons: (1) my father, the groundskeeper, responded poorly to finding paths worn into his lawn and they showed more when they were worn into snow, and (2) it got dark sooner.

As soon as it got dark, The Man Who Hid in the Shed got his powers. He could leap out at any time and snag an unsuspecting dishwasher and God only knew what happened after that. The possibilities lurking in the gravel pit after dark, for a child with an imagination as vivid as mine, were overwhelming in their sheer number, much less their scope. Sometimes they would just loom up out of the darkness and overtake me like a particularly virulent genie.

More than once my father would be standing in the kitchen, wondering idly how many children he really had and whatever happened to the one who used to wash dishes, when the back door would fly open and his oldest child—carrying one plate— would fly through it as if she had been chased the last forty feet by a pack of rabid wolves. Her eyes would be wide and frightened, her breathing would be labored, her cheeks would be a deep scarlet, as if she had been outside in the cold for perhaps hours, for some unknown reason she would be carrying one dinner plate and a spatula.

This man and this child hardly ever spoke to each other and they never spoke of these things. The man never spoke because she was over the age of six and under the age of twenty-five and therefore a total enigma to him. The child never spoke because she had been told he knew everything, saw everything, had a firm opinion about everything and all of these impressions and opinions just happened to coincide exactly with impressions and opinions of her mother. They were a united front, her parents, of one opinion, one mind: and since he was not all that talkative, she had no real conflicting information. She would not know for another fifteen years that when he shook his head and walked back into the living room to watch television it was not disapproval as much as blind confusion, nor would she understand for those same fifteen years that he was no more like her mother than she was.

Still, I held my ground. It was not fair. I was the only child in the family with an assigned task that lasted, as near as I could tell, until the end of time. Not only did I have to drop my own life to baby-sit whenever my parents chose to go off gallivanting— which, since my mother was a square-dance caller and therefore a critical member of several square-dance clubs, they did every Friday and Saturday night—but I had to wash dishes every day for seven people.

S-E-V-E-N.

My mother, who cleaned house, did the laundry and cooked for seven people, was peculiarly unsympathetic. My lesser siblings shot away from the dinner table like rockets, on the off chance the responsibility might shift without warning.

I have a vague but persistent memory of the Wee One wandering out to visit me in my exile in the kitchen, apparently driven by the need to make useless conversation, and remarking, "I like to wash dishes, don't you, Sherry?" It's a wonder the child lived.

I have never liked to wash dishes. I don't like to cook because it creates dirty dishes that then just sit around, needing to be washed. I do it now, though. Sometimes I even feign a smile and good cheer. I can washes dishes in about the same amount of time it takes anyone else to wash them.

Or, I can also make the task last all day, it just depends on what kind of mood I'm in or where I think The Man Who Hid in the Shed might be hiding now.

mother learns to swim

WHEN I WAS four years old my father took me to a large body of water and threw me in, and when I came up shrieking and grabbing for air he said, "Good—she can swim." We have no idea how many children there should have been in our family. He only kept the five that were waterproof. The only non-swimmer in our family was our mother, who spent most of the leisure hours of our youth either back on shore, or in the boat, her hand welding their own grips in the gunwales as we raced and swooped around the chain of lakes where we played.

Our mother was a confirmed non-swimmer. She didn't like to get her face wet. She hated to be splashed. She was happiest about ankle deep with a fearless toddler to guard, conveniently preventing her from coming out into the depths where the rest of us were. By the time the youngest among us was born, I was a certified junior lifesaver and the UnWee and the Wee One were both better swimmers than I was; we took it upon ourselves to free our mother by teaching the baby to swim. He was a large, happy, round baby who never talked until he was three and never walked until he was four—both because he never had any reason. Since he was carried everywhere he went anyway, he never seemed to notice he was in water. We would play with him until we became bored and then just float him like a small air mattress. When he started to drift away, someone would reach out and grab a foot or his hair and pull him back to us. The baby loved it. It seemed perfectly natural to us. Citing his continued need to survive his siblings, however, our mother signed up, at the age of about thirty-four, for swimming lessons.

This seemed fairly foolish to us. We had all taken swimming lessons. Every summer for as long as we could remember we had been thrust into our suits, issued beach bags with our names on the outside and our clean underwear to change into and a towel on the inside, and ferried to the beach for swimming lessons. Although I was not a lesbian at the time and would not become one for another twenty years, I learned to get my face wet voluntarily to please my beauty queen/lifeguard teacher, Delores. I would have dog-paddled to China for Delores. At the time our mother learned to swim I could swim the required ten body lengths under water and both the UnWee and the Wee One could dive off one shore of the lake and come up on the other. We felt qualified to teach.

Mom's first lesson was to get her face wet. This is a huge stepping-stone for non-swimmers, but for children who dove out of the car, raced down the beach and plunged headfirst into untested waters, it was a difficult trauma to take seriously. I offered to look up Delores because she was such a fine teacher, but Mom took offense. She was embarrassed because she could not swim. She had, after all, watched us do it fairly fearlessly for years. This did not help our cause in any way. We would take her to the beach to "practice," offer to dunk her ourselves, dissolve into gales of laughter over our own cleverness and then run for our wicked little lives. One just did not make fun of our mother.

Her second lesson that I remember was to float. After years of observation and experimentation, I have surmised that stick-shaped people float like rocks. As I have gained stature and dimension throughout my life, I have gone from floating easily to bobbing like a cork, and while stick-shaped people have to struggle to stay on top of the water, I now struggle to get completely wet. However, my mother was never a stick. All she needed, I assured her, was faith. All I needed, she assured me, was to go to the far end of the lake and float until I was blue in the face. Like fine wine, she would float in her own time. I pointed out that she was old already, which was received nearly as graciously as my offer to find Delores.

When she did float, she would stiffen like a board and slap herself against the water and then come up spluttering and swearing that it could not be done, that there was some peculiar physical property to her body that would not allow it to float. "You're too tense, Mom, you need to relax," we would reassure her as we all floated supportively around her, and then we would dive under water, where we were relatively safe.

Eventually, after much swearing, a lot of frustration and an occasional bout of tears, Mother became proficient enough in water that she passed her beginning swimming class. She could swim. The morning after she passed her test she woke up an expert in all forms of water navigation. She had confidence. I had no idea, she told me, what it was like to overcome fear at her age. I was young. I had never been afraid of water. I had no idea what she had accomplished.

And she was right: I had no fear of the water. I swam with the unquestioned belief that I could swim my way out of any situation. I had been dunked, I had fallen off skis and catapulted to the bottom of the lake, I had been dragged by a towrope once; and while each of these experiences had frightened me at the time, I still found myself baffled over exactly how anyone could drown. It did not compute. I took junior lifesaving, where our teacher patiently and repeatedly told us how dangerous drowning people can be, how even if we knew how to do rescues and we knew how to do them safely, we should always always AL-WAYS stop and evaluate the risks before we dove in. What they taught me repeatedly in junior lifesaving is that the only thing more tragic than one person drowning is two people drowning.

To celebrate her new success and to practice her newfound skill, my mother took us to the beach. I wandered out to the diving dock and dove off, and was effortlessly floating in the water just beyond the dock, mulling over swimming out to the raft or just staying where I was. I was floating upright, like a cork, a position I could maintain for hours with just an occasional underwater sweep of my hand. I no doubt looked utterly relaxed. I may have looked like I was standing shoulder deep in water, although the water was about seven feet deep.

My mother called, "Look out, Sherry, here I come," and ran and cannonballed into the water.

I had just enough time to think, "Why . . . ?"

Her head popped up out of the water right beside me, her eyes bugged, she went "Uhhhh . . ." inhaling half the lake, and she went under, and as she went, she grabbed me.

I grabbed the dock on the way down: had I been any farther away, I would have been in a fight for my life. Everything I had learned—and had practiced, repeatedly—about how to get out of the grip of a drowning person was erased with the initial shock. She grabbed me and shoved me underwater as she struggled to climb over me to reach the surface. The strength of her grip, the unreasoning, flailing force of her panic was superhuman.

I grabbed the dock, hauled her up to it, and managed to latch her onto it instead of me while she hung and coughed and spluttered and choked and eventually cleared her airway. When she recovered, she was furious with me. I had "tricked" her. I should have told her the water was over her head. When I mentioned the incident a few years later as an example of how swiftly survival can become an issue in the water, she was angry again, claiming that I exaggerated, that she had never really panicked, that she would have been fine.

Mom became an adequate swimmer, but she never became the kind of fearless waterbabies that we were. She could tolerate it, but she never really liked to get her face wet. She reached a certain comfort level that assured her that if any of us got into trouble in the water, she could wade in and help us out.

And while I would never have taken that confidence away from her, it was she who taught me just how dangerous that assurance can be.

my ten most beautiful things

IN FOURTH GRADE I was an unfinished work. I loved school and, because I craved attention and approval, I did well there. I was a sponge soaking up praise and reassurance from any source that would offer it; while I was not a popular student among my peers, I was a chronic overachiever in the classroom. My specialties—and this had already been noticed— were those things that came most easily to me. The first time I ever genuinely broke a sweat over a textbook was in an economics class my junior year in college just after I transferred to U of M. The first fourteen years of school I majored in my Great Potential with a minor in Con Artistry. I had a way with words. It was—and remains—my sole survival skill, and it came to me perhaps too easily. It did not come, however, without a price.

I liked my fourth-grade teacher. She was that unfathomable age that all grade school teachers are, somewhere between parents and angels. She liked me. I had extraordinary luck with teachers all through grade school—I only had one who did not actively like me, and she tolerated me remarkably well. I was quite comfortable in fourth grade. I sat in the middle of the room, near the front, I raised my hand to answer every question, I loved going up to the board . . . I floundered somewhat in math, but I never expected to use it much anyway. I excelled in reading. I did well in a fairly useless class we had called "English." I wasn't even paying attention the afternoon our teacher told us we had to write a poem: the subject was to be My Ten Most Beautiful Things.

I did not pour my heart and soul into this poem. I diddled around in class, whispering to my best friend until we got caught, and five minutes before class ended I scribbled some stuff on my paper and handed it in. My poem was titled "My Ten Most Beautiful Things" because that was the assignment.

Our teacher was so impressed by my poem that she took me aside to tell me mine was the best in the class. She had me read it to the class. My class was impressed as much as any group of fourth graders are impressed by poetry. Our teacher told me she liked my poem so much she was going to have it PUBLISHED.

I went home and told my mom. One of my ten most beautiful things was "A cardinal overhead." Another was "My mother in a new dress." My mother liked my poem, too.

I particularly liked the fame and attention my poem gave me. It had been sheer accident and I knew it, but praise was praise and no one loved praise like I did. I reveled in it. I rolled in it like a dog in new grass. I would sit in class and think back on my poem and remind myself how incredibly—even if accidentally—good I was.

A few days after our teacher told me she was going to have my poem published, she called me aside and told me the school PRINCIPAL wanted to talk to me.

I was beginning to sense there might be no end to my fame.

The principal was substitute teaching in the sixth-grade class.

Sixth graders were gods.

There were no mortal beings on earth as important, as powerful, as awesome as sixth graders. After sixth grade they just fell off the edge of earth, into something called "Junior High" and there was no way of knowing what happened to them after that—but in my school, sixth graders ruled. To even be seen with a sixth grader could make you automatically more important: to actually know one was to touch the hem of God.

To report to the principal, I had to walk in on a class of thirty-five studying sixth graders, up to her oversized teacher's desk, and still be able to talk.

She was expecting me. She told me she had read my poem.

I felt more confident; I was going to get more praise.

She told me my poem was very good.

I thanked her demurely.

She asked me if there were anything about my poem I would like to tell her.

I had scribbled that poem off in the last five minutes of class without giving it two thoughts; I would have been lucky to have been able to tell her what was in it, much less to share any in-depth thoughts about it.

She said, "This poem is awfully good for a fourth grader, don't you think?"

I said, "What?"

She said, "Are you sure you didn't just read this somewhere, Cheryl?"

I had not yet made the connection between poetry and Mother Goose rhymes—I had never intentionally read a poem in my life. On the other hand, I had just scribbled that work of art off in the last five minutes of class—in my fourth-grade heart, I had no way of knowing where the inspiration had come from and I did not, at the time, fully understand her question. I answered, "No," but without the same self-assurance I had had when the conversation started.

She said, "Because I think you might have read this poem somewhere before, and then turned it in in class, not realizing that is stealing."

I stood there, in front of thirty-five allegedly studying sixth graders, and I could not think of a word to say.

It had never occurred to me that there might be a penalty for being too good at something.

It had never occurred to me to steal a poem.

She told me that if I promised her I had written that poem by myself, she would take my word for it.

I promised her. I knew it was a trick, one of those adult things, and I knew she didn't believe me, but hell would have frozen over before I would have let her know what I knew.

I went back to my fourth-grade class utterly crushed. I was convinced I had done something terribly wrong, but I could not isolate exactly what. All I truly understood from my conversation with the principal was that she did not believe that I was good enough. Single-handedly in a ten-minute conversation she had erased all of the confidence and self-assurance my teacher had spent the school year trying to help me build.

I went home and told my mother that the principal thought I had read my poem somewhere.

I understand all hell broke loose shortly after that.

My mother had no tolerance for thieves and even less for people who abused their authority, but God save the authority figure who unjustly accused one of HER children of stealing.

I understand an in-person discussion was held.

I was not invited.

It must have been an interesting discussion, however, because after it took place the principal was a stickler for discipline for every student in her school but one. Had I been just a little bit sharper or a little less bent on winning every adult's approval, I might have made that woman's life miserable for a good two years. She went out of her way to make mine uneventful.

My teacher had had no idea why our principal had wanted to see me and she told me personally that she would never have sent me if she had known. She took great pains to explain to me that the principal had been wrong and had behaved badly.

I was groomed for most of my educational life to become a teacher. It was, for the women who taught me, a safe, respectable way for a woman to make a living. As we boomer women were told over and over again, before the statistics finally made themselves felt, we could always count on nursing or teaching to support ourselves. I assumed I would be a teacher myself for a long time, but when it came down to taking those niggling education classes that were supposed to earn my bread and butter, I sat down and I had a long private chat with myself. I isolated a few facts I had been ignoring: (1) I didn't like children when I was one. I'm not ready to sell them into slavery to pay off my taxes, and I do like the occasional bright child, but as a group—they are not my favorites. (2) I don't really like teaching. I like having knowledge; I like showing off my knowledge; I even like sharing my knowledge; I do not have that selfless desire to see small minds grow. (3) Not a single soul who knows me has ever admired me for my patience.

I am forty-eight years old. Whenever I have written something I am particularly proud of, and I have shared it with a few friends who have admired it, and I have milked everyone around me for as much praise as they can possibly give, and someone less familiar reads it and that person says—as if surprised—*You know*—*this is really good* . . . I can still see those thirty-five sixth graders pretending to read.

I only had one teacher who truly did not understand children and I only had her for less than fifteen minutes. I know what a difference a good teacher can make.

moomeries

ABOUT A YEAR AGO my good truck Hopalong and I were cruising slowly along the gravel road that runs behind Southern Michigan Prison, hunting for deer, when I espied, in the road ahead of me, an escaped inmate. The inmate looked at me and slowly chewed whatever it is inmates chew. I looked at the inmate. He was way too big to be anyone I wanted to deal with, so I drove away immediately to the nearest State Police post (located conveniently right next to the prison) and reported that steer #43 had jumped the fence. He was now standing on the edge of the road ruminating about his newfound freedom. At the rate he was fleeing, I reported, they would have three or four hours to run out and catch him before he crossed the road. The officer thanked me for being a good citizen, showed me a map so I could pinpoint the scene of the crime, and said they would send someone out. I avoided the area for several days just to be on the safe side—I've met hostile Angus before.

My life has been punctuated by testy relationships with cattle.

In fact, I have not done well with anything sporting cloven hooves. When I was very, very small, my parents employed a twelve-foot goat to torment me. Her name was Suzy and she lived in the Suzy House, which, before Suzy, had been a small milk house attached to the barn in our back yard. When Suzy moved in she spent a great deal of her time creating small brown beads, which she used to decorate her new home. I could not have been much more than three or four when Suzy lived with us, so bits and pieces of my memories are missing—most notably, how I repeatedly came so close to an animal I hated so passionately—but I spent much of my early youth pinned to the ground in the back yard under my parents' goat while she stood on the straps of my bibs and ate my hair. She was big and ugly and she smelled bad. Eventually she ate all of the grass in her pen and my father began chaining her to a cement block, which she dutifully dragged all over the neighborhood until one night he came home and found her standing on the roof of his car (I don't remember, offhand, where the block was) and she mysteriously disappeared.

My middle sister, the UnWee, is a woman of firm and determined opinions. A few years ago she bought a new house and while I was searching for a housewarming present I asked her what she needed or would like. She said, "Anything but a cow." I admired her resolve, but assured her I rarely present urban dwellers with livestock as housewarming gifts. She was unmoved. She came to the city to get away from cows, she assured me; she did not want any cows in her back yard. She did not want any cows in her life. (This is probably why she moved to Old Dairy Farm Road.) She did not want any cows on her refrigerator, or her cookie jar, or her dish towels. Any likeness of a cow, the UnWee told me, would be unwelcome in her home. She plans to live her life in a cow-free environment. Reassured, I took her out for a steak.

The UnWee has reason to be bitter: she was forced to quit school in kindergarten during The Great Cow War. Our mother was summoned to the school and spoken to by the teacher because the UnWee had rolled up her nap blanket and gone to wait for the bus. The UnWee informed our mother that the teacher had told the entire class that ONLY BULLS HAVE HORNS. The UnWee, who had only recently been treated to the sight of thirty (female) cows staggering around in a bloody daze because they had been de-horned, knew her teacher was too dumb to teach anything the UnWee cared to learn. It took some persuasion from our mother to convince her that knowledge extends beyond basic farm lore and that perhaps even city folk know things five-year-olds do not.

I (the Least Wee), the UnWee and the Wee One (and two smaller brothers we never bother to count) all lived in a farmhouse with no farm. Someone had dug it up and carried it away as gravel so rather than being surrounded by farmland we were surrounded by a huge hole in the ground, which included two big ponds. When we were very young, there was a huge barn at the back of our lot and it was to this barn that the Suzy House was attached. Having abandoned his profession as a goatherder, our father briefly penned in a few calves around the barn, had his picture taken with them and then apparently sold them. My father never wanted to be a farmer. He had grown up on a small dairy farm; his life had been dictated from five in the morning until whenever he finished at night, seven days a week, for twenty years, by the milking schedule of a herd of ungrateful Guernseys, and he was done. He fought briefly with the farming gene, first with Suzy, then with the calves, and I think he was relieved when our landlord came over one day and towed away the barn. The barn, as I remember it, was huge, a haymow in the middle, with milking stanchions and the milk house at one end, and a few animal pens on the other. One day a group of men came, shored up the beams, picked up the whole barn, set it on a frame with wheels, and drove away with it. I can still see that barn moving slowly down the road, the rural answer to mobile homes.

My father's parents were dairy farmers, my mother's parents did a variety of things—my grandfather was a retired railroadman—but, having survived the Great Depression, they maintained a garden, a barn, several fields and two cows. When the economy fell apart again, the banks crashed and all of the rich people killed themselves, my grandparents would manage, once again, to survive. This was my grandmother's explanation of why she kept two cows she never seemed to like, and for years I believed everyone kept cows as insurance against the next Great Depression, which could happen anytime the Democrats were elected. I felt much safer when, as a child, I was given a grocery sack full of baby ducks, because I knew I was at least six ducks away from starvation and suicide myself. I asked my mother why we didn't keep two cows in case Democrats were elected and the Great Depression came back and my mother muttered words she told ME never to use.

My mother's parents' two cows were a Holstein and a Guernsey. For city folk, that is a big black-and-white cow and a big red-and-white cow. Both give milk. As I recall, the Holstein was so large she could barely make it through the barn door, which apparently worried her too, because she always did it at a dead run. I avoided her. Particularly, I avoided being in the same barn doorway with her. I believe her name was "Petunia." The Guernsey was named "Junie." Petunia annoyed my grandmother at great length because she would only eat the grass on the far side of the fence, and, being a big cow, she did this by simply leaning against the fence until it gave up and let her over. She preferred to effect these escapes on or near the railroad tracks that ran along the edge of my grandparents' property; because my grandfather had worked for the railroad, this posed a particularly strong sense of responsibility for them. I don't believe Petunia ever actually attacked a train, but she certainly kept my grandmother alert and fit.

I never felt entirely safe at my grandparents' farm. My father's parents kept about thirty Guernseys. Guernseys are not small cows and they don't get any smaller when there are thirty of them. When my sisters and I spent the night with my grandparents, we would be sent down the lane in the morning to fetch the cows. This is much like sending mice to find a flock of eagles. The cows would be standing around the woods at the end of the lane, waiting for small children to trample, and when we appeared they would lower their heads, study us intently, turn to each other, and give the signal: "MOOOOOooo." I would then turn and run like the wind for the barn with thirty cows galloping along behind me. Among my fondest childhood memories this rates right up next to my aunt's favorite game, called, "No, YOU test the electric fence . . ." My aunt was five years older than I was, and she believed quite firmly that I was a useless pain in her backside—her response to that challenge was to electrocute me.

When we got the cows up to the barn, they each had a specific stanchion they plodded to be milked. Occasionally brief territorial battles would break out over whose stanchion was whose, which would cause my grandfather to snarl, "Hey," and slap his cows with a pitchfork. My sisters and I never argued in front of him. The cows would then be locked by the neck into their stanchions where they ate and were milked at the same time. My grandfather's cows never appeared to truly enjoy being milked. Periodically they would kick at the milking machines, or jerk around as if trying to pull their udders free, and every once in a while they would let a hind foot fly back in search of small children. Their favorite amusement, however, was to wait until someone ordered a small child to deliver something at the far end of the barn, load their tails up with used cowfeed and then WHAP the child in the face with it as they sidled by. Cow tails are made of hairs of about the consistency of fishline and when delivered with just the right touch they sting like mad. This is probably why flies don't like them.

I lived in terror of being bitten by a cow for years. This amused my grandparents and my aunt to no end, which made me feel abused and misunderstood, but the most reassurance I ever got was, "No cow bite is gonna hurt you." Eventually I strayed too close to a calf just before feeding time and while I was trying to pet him, he ate my hand. He clamped down good and hard and set up a sucking motion that was impressive, and I was about to set up a shrieking action that would be just as impressive, if not more so, when I realized IT DIDN'T HURT. Cows only have upper teeth: apparently it doesn't take more than that to pluck grass. So when my greatest cow fear came to pass, I did not lose my arm to the elbow, I was just slimed.

Still. Cows Get Out.

Whenever we were at our grandparents', the UnWee, the Wee One and I lived in terror of the inevitable: someone would appear out of nowhere and report breathlessly, "The Cows Are Out!" When we were very small, we would be ushered into the house and ordered to stay there until someone came to get us— and we immediately presumed that might, in fact, be the cows, having killed all of the adults. . . . I still have nightmares about the cows Getting Out, breaking into my grandparents' house, stampeding up the stairs after me and looking into the trunk where I am hiding. . . . When we were older, we were ordered OUTSIDE and told to stand in front of the flower gardens and wave our arms. In a cattle stampede we were expected to risk our lives to protect the begonias.

We had all seen *Rawhide*.

All of this came back to me the day I gazed through Hopalong's windshield and discovered inmate #43 and I were on the same side of the fence. He was Out. He was big. He was bovine. He had the same flat, stupid eyes I remember from my childhood. I drove away in a flash, thinking, "To hell with the begonias . . ."

Let some convict chase cows.

the atlantic and pacific tea company

My Grandmother Molby did all of her trading at the Atlantic and Pacific Tea Company. I often went along to trade with her because it summoned up notions of wearing hides and feathers and swapping tobacco for firewater (neither of which I had or even remotely needed) and because we always came out with M&M's. She knew all of the checkout people by name and they all knew her. One—Alice—had grown up with my Aunt Janette and had become a career checkout clerk. It was an admirable career, not one anyone took lightly. When I was in high school, checkout clerks were rumored to make almost as much per hour as employees at GM.

My grandmother was not that far removed from the generation when one really did walk into the Atlantic and Pacific Tea Company, slap down fifteen animal pelts, six dozen eggs and four billion tomatoes and use them as tender for those exotic things one could not grow or catch on one's own—tea, for instance. My grandmother could have traded hollyhocks, poppies, roses and gladiolas for M&M's, but I never actually saw her do it.

When I went to the A&P with my grandmother, I was always allowed to bask in the glory of my heritage. Old women who seemed to know my grandmother would walk up to us and say, "Well—this must be Eloise's daughter," and I would smile and squirm self-consciously. That I was that easily recognized by people I did not know but who knew my elders had not yet become problematic.

So we did our trading at the A&P and then we carried the M&M's home and put them away, and then we cleaned house, and then we made and ate supper and washed the dishes and carried out the trash and then we sat down to watch Groucho Marx abuse George Fenneman. My grandmother hated Groucho Marx, and fussed about him for the entire half-hour he was on, every time he was on, for as long as he was on. Then she went to the kitchen and came back with three bowls, one for me, one for her, and one for my grandfather, and we had M&M's. My grandmother and I would use the various colors to make floral arrangements in the bottoms of our bowls, while my grandfather would just scoop them up by the handful and eat them. We felt morally superior to him. We were more aesthetic. We would frequently discuss our moral and aesthetic superiority in his presence, but I don't know that he even heard us. Certainly our conversations never affected the way he ate M&M's.

I often stayed over at my grandmother's house. There was no plan or pattern to it. She would come to our house bearing old copies of *The Ladies' Home Journal*, *Redbook*, *Family Circle*, and *Reader's Digest*. Either she or my Aunt Janette brought us *National Geographic*. She brought us flowers all summer that she had grown in her yard. She brought us peas and beans and tomatoes and strawberries. She brought us dress patterns and fabric and dresses pinned together to be measured and fitted. And then she would decide to go home and one of my sisters or I would decide to go with her.

My grandmother was a stately woman, about five feet six inches, a stout woman, a large and powerful and safe woman.

Unless she was going to town she always wore an apron and she always smelled faintly of soap. Dirt and disorder in any form lived in mortal fear of my grandmother. Dust mites in other people's houses went scurrying off under the furniture to get away from her. She did not tolerate disorder in her own life and she did not tolerate disorder in the lives of those she loved. She did not tolerate it particularly well in the neighbor's dogs.

When I was eleven I was standing in the dining room of her house on M-86 and I was flipping through either *Look* or *Life* magazine while she and my mother talked and I discovered an article about an eleven-year-old girl in India who had just had a baby. Worried this might be contagious, I read on that this girl had said the father was a twenty-one-year-old soldier currently off fighting a war. I read this information to my mother and I asked, "How does she know who the father is?" My mother got one of those I-should-have-been-childless expressions on her face, but my grandmother never hesitated: she looked up at me and she said, "Just never you mind."

Her hair always fascinated me. She did not cut it until she was well into her eighties and the strain of keeping it up just became too wearing. When I was a child I used to sit and watch her comb it each morning when she got up and each evening before she went to bed. It fell down over her shoulders, down her back, past the stool where she sat and nearly touched the floor. She was in her early sixties when I was born and the strain of her life had taken its toll, so her hair was quite thin, but the length, nonetheless, made me envious. During the day she always wore it up in a bun on the back of her head, and while I knew her, the hair around her face faded from dark gray into silver, but the bun on the back of her head stayed brown.

We went to the A&P on Tuesdays. I don't know why she selected that particular day as opposed to any other, but I do know that she lived and shopped as if she lived fifty miles by oxcart from the nearest store. During the time I knew her, the farthest she ever lived from the A&P was four miles. She just did not go to town often. Going to town was an event. It required preparation. One had to look one's best. She always combed her hair. She always touched up her makeup, pancake makeup which she wore to cover blemishes in her complexion, the only makeup she ever wore. She always wore a clean, freshly pressed dress. It came out of the closet pressed and she pressed it again.

In fact, she always wore a dress. According to my mother, when she baled hay, which is a hot, dusty, scratchy, thankless job, she pulled on my grandfather's coveralls over her dress; but she gardened in a dress; she mucked out stalls in a dress; she tended her chickens in a dress—she even killed them in a dress. She had one dress pattern from which she made every dress I ever saw her wear, so the question when we saw her drive in was not what she was wearing, but whether it was navy-and-white-dotted Swiss, brown-and-white-dotted Swiss, navy small-print cotton gingham, brown small-print cotton gingham, or navy-and-white gingham plaid, or brown-and-white . . . And once she had made a dress, she wore it until the spots fell out. My grandmother got the last possible drop of use out of everything she ever owned.

She wore a "good" dress to go to town. She carried her purse, which opened with a clasp at the top and swung by the straps from her forearm and which had a snap/latch on the inside to hold her car keys. If she ever bought a new purse it must have looked just exactly like the old purse because I only remember one.

The clothes she made for us—and she made nearly all of them—reflected her values, if not necessarily her private tastes. She built dresses for active children who lived in their clothes, dresses with triple stitching between the blouse and the skirt and reinforced stitching to hold on the sleeves. As soon as I discovered style and popular fashion these dresses became the bane of my existence. They were homemade. They were indestructible. The first store-bought dress I ever owned I wore during a rousing game of trucks and, scooting around on my hands and knees on the floor, I ripped the skirt right off the blouse, an accident unimaginable in one of my grandmother's dresses. Much to my mortification she bought a new sewing machine that boasted a raft of decorative stitches and I was compelled to appear before my peers in dresses with rows and rows and rows of machine-sewn ducks and snowflakes and whirly-gigs. No one else wore dresses like that. I would walk into my class and my schoolmates would smile and say, "Oh, your grandmother made you a new dress." Older now, I think perhaps I heard the criticism in my own head and missed a more subtle, kinder message.

She did use more than one pattern for our dresses, however, and she certainly used more than two colors. Our clothes were color-coded for us to reflect our personalities and tastes. Nearly everything she made for the UnWee was blue, while the Wee One was decked in bright yellows and I was ensconced—until I finally objected—in a sea of pink. But she made us beautiful clothes. I remember a shirtwaist dress of polished cotton she made for me that was a coppery brown with pink piping and a row of pink set in down the sides of the front placket; and an ivory polished cotton dress with a drop-waist and pastel flowers in the print . . . One of my favorite dresses of all time featured the much-hated rows of fancy machine-stitching down the front. I believe we compromised on the number of rows of ducks. Our dresses were beautiful. Not necessarily the cutting edge of fashion at the time, but each and every one of them was a work of love.

On the way into town to the A&P we would pass the abandoned buildings around the cement factory where, once upon a time, the Dagos had lived. They had all come over here—many from Italy—to work and live in the cement plant, and then it closed. So they all moved downtown and bought ice cream parlors. As I remember that story, there was a point to it, some sort of life lesson about struggle and hard work, but it's gone now. My grandfather spent hours smoking his cigar and telling me stories about the railroad, the job he had before the Depression, the kinds of jobs on the railroad he had during the Depression, the railroad lines and where they went and who owned them and who bought them and the freight that was shipped and Chicago, Toledo, Baltimore, Philadelphia . . . and what I remember of these long, historically rich ramblings is one word—*Nickleplate*. It sounded funny. I was sitting at a train crossing years later watching the cars fly past and there, written on the side of one, was the word—*Nickleplate*. I was so excited I nearly drove into the side of it.

My grandmother was a wealth of information about the community where I grew up. I had only to point to a house and she would frown and say, "I don't know who lives there now," and then she would tell me everything she knew about the five families who had lived there before, whose son had been killed in World War II, whose daughter married a Catholic and was never seen not pregnant again, whose second cousin had married that so-and-so boy and was living in the white house down on the corner of Behnke Road and Wherever Street . . . She told me about the little ten-year-old girl named Mary who was playing in the barn, swinging on the rope between the hay lofts and who fell and died; she told me about taking care of her father when he was old and infirm and not himself; she told me about driving the horse-and-buggy when she was a kid because her mother didn't like to. She told me that before the war she drove a "big old Buick" that was so high off the road she once drove over a full-grown pig and both the Buick and the pig survived. She told me her mother owned a photography shop when my grandmother was a little girl in the 1890s. She told me about the cats she had

had in her life, Buster and Teddy and Timmy. I don't remember the stories she told. Fragments. Pieces here and there. What I remember, in retrospect, is a sense of connectedness and of history. A complex interweaving of people and lives and changes and luck and hard work and courage that winding in all around each other made up a family and beyond that, a community.

Always a woman concerned about keeping busy and being useful, she was more than anxious to be on her way when she died at the age of ninety-four. I find her memories in curious places. In the faces of poppies . . . The scent of a rose . . . But her stories are buried in my heart and every now and then as I go about my normal life a proud old cat who died before I was ever born will brush against my leg, or a big old Buick will run over an angry and ruffled pig and I will look up and find myself standing beside a coffee grinder, inhaling the strong, nostalgic smell of fresh-ground coffee—and once again I am five years old and doing my trading with my grandmother at the A&P.

litter string

THERE IS A GOLD PAW hanging out of the fan box. It is July, 110 degrees in the shade, his Mommy is sitting in the direct path of the floor fan in front of the computer where she is sipping iced tea by the half gallon and thinking wistfully of the lake and Babycakes is napping inside the fan box. He needs his shelter— the only rooms in the house that are even TOLERABLE with all of this stifling heat happen also to have those big, noisy boxes in the window that shove wind across his delicate whiskers and ruffle his coat . . .

He is uncommonly fond of boxes. When he was young he and Mommy played a game called "Seal the Box." Mommy would remove the lid from a big plastic box and Babycakes would jump in and make himself at home, then Mommy would put the lid on top of the box. He would wait patiently because he trusted his Mommy and soon she would remove the frustration and he would jump out . . . stretch . . . and jump back into the box. He once played Seal the Box at a party Mommy gave for her friends. Mommy sealed him in the box and then went where the air changes. Babycakes waited patiently. When Mommy came back, a small circle of her close, personal friends had gathered in around the box and were saying things to themselves, like, "Do you really think she put him in there?" "Can he get any air?" "My wife would kill me if I did something like that." Mommy removed the frustration and—with the slow, methodical grace of a born ham, Babycakes stood up, stretched, and stepped daintily out of the box . . . He spent the rest of the party helping the guest of honor unwrap birthday presents.

Babycakes loves wrapping paper. Last year when Mommy came home with boxes and began hiding them all with wrapping paper, Mommy gave Babycakes an entire roll of his own. She said, "Play with this before I kill you," which is Mommy's way of saying, "You're the best cat I've ever had, Babycakes, and I love you more than life itself."

Babycakes loves string, although string can turn on you. String just hangs there, taunting you, wriggling its very tip to entice you from time to time . . . A long piece of string Mommy hangs from her window attacked Babycakes once, wrapped around his hind end, and followed him under the coffee table, around the leg and back around another leg, all the while squeezing Babycakes tighter and tighter, making him very unhappy that he had ever played with that string at all. Before the string attack, there were strings hanging from every window in the house, but Mommy went around and tied them all up in knots that Babycakes can barely reach anymore. However, she was kind enough to hang some strings from her coat, which he understood were for his pleasure. She tied one to her nightgown once too, but something happened to it.

She hangs long, wide strings from the wall in the room where she keeps her litterbox as well, but once Babycakes tried to help her play with that string and she howled and told him he was the spawn of Satan. Mommy is touchy when she's in her litterbox. Babycakes used to like paper bags. They were exactly the right size for his being. A young cat could curl up inside a paper bag and sleep to his heart's content, while outside Mommy would wander the length and breadth of the house calling, "Babycakes . . . Babycakes . . ." When he had concluded his work he would step out of his bag, yawn and shatter Mommy's nerves. This was great fun for a young cat, but one day he stepped out of his bag and it followed him. He stepped again: again the bag followed. This seemed wrong to him, so he decided to leave—but the bag filled up with air and began making horrid, terrifying flapping noises, and still IT WENT EVERYWHERE HE WENT. He ran right, he ran left, he did his best leaps and turns and turning leaps, and still the blasted bag followed him and at that moment, that nanosecond that contained the greatest terror of his life, his own MOMMY grabbed him by his perfect coat, forced him to lay down AGAINST his will and said, "You stuck your head through the handle, stupid."

No one had EVER called Babycakes "stupid" before.

It was all the bag's fault.

The only good bag is a dead bag.

The best ones to kill are the plastic ones Mommy fills with trash and then ties at the top—if you catch one just right and run and jump on it hard enough, sometimes it goes "Poof!" and makes a lot of bag noise. Then Mommy says bad words and comes and puts it all in another bag.

But best of all Babycakes likes boxes. He likes boxes with an open door. He likes boxes of all sizes, but he loves boxes that are just a little bigger than he is. He balls up inside his box with his head—or just one paw—poking out, guaranteeing free egress, and he does his most serious work of the day. And he needs his rest, because Mommy doesn't understand life at all, and if it weren't for him, she would never catnap and she would sleep ALL NIGHT LONG!

A good Mommy would let him play with her soft, white litter string.

She's very lucky to have him.

She should probably stop threatening to throw him out with the trash.

fat girls and lawn chairs

Due to the wear and tear of aging, I have lost half an inch in height. I have mourned that half an inch because—in my mind—it was the half inch that kept me from being as wide as I am tall. Back when I still had this half an inch and thought of myself as tall and lithe, I happened into a mall bathroom where, as I emerged from the stall, a teenaged girl was scowling critically at her reflection in the mirror. Disgusted with herself, she grasped the roll of fat that was hanging disgracefully over the belt of her size four jeans and she wailed to her friends, "I am SUCH a cow . . ." And then she saw me. That a size four child is distressed because her babyfat won't stay inside her jeans is probably not all that funny: but the stunned panic on her face when she saw me warned me that I was either going to have to laugh at her or kill her. I walked out of the restroom chuckling about a herd of tiny size four cows.

I have a friend who is smaller than I am. Several, actually: but I know this particular friend is smaller than I am because she gave me all of her "fat" clothes. Not all of them fit. She had been biking, hiking, golfing and starving herself into a thinner, more athletic image, and like many of us who are zaftig, she was in a "thin" period. This was, admittedly, a few years ago. The passion that kept her moving and hungry apparently burned out, and like me, she has been eating her Wheaties. She still probably is smaller than I am. This might matter to me or to her, but it is probably splitting some very fine hairs as far as our thinner friends can tell. But after a weekend outing, I now have the reputation for being the thinner of the two of us by the grace of a lawn chair.

I was once small enough to fit comfortably in the lap of a lawn chair. I think smaller people probably take lawn chairs for granted, but that is because they have never been hugged in the butt by The Thing That Won't Let Go. And they have never had the experience that scarred my friend.

We'll call her Kristen. It's a pretty name and it's not hers. Kristen brought a lawn chair to a gathering of our friends. It was a weekend outing, a long holiday in which we conspired to gather at someone's cottage, float around the lake on rafts, eat massive quantities of food and describe this adventure by some obscure athletic event that at least half of us participated in. We call it "The Canoe Trip." This distinguishes it from "The Cross Country Ski Trip" where we gather at the lodge, float around in the Jacuzzi, eat massive quantities of food and some of us even go outside.

My friend Kristen was quite proud of her lawn chair. It was new. It was cute. It was a steal. Kristen is a woman who enjoys her toys, and it was a lawn chair to inspire the envy of all of her friends. She set up her lawn chair on the deck, arranged her towel, her drink, and the direction she was facing, and then she sat down. And the lawn chair, which was inexpensive and probably made by Chinese—none of whom are notably large people—began to spread out on the deck, spraddle-legged like a giraffe on ice, and slowly—excruciatingly slowly—it lowered her utterly without escape or grace until she was flat on her

fat girls and lawn chairs
155

butt on the deck, the wounded chair parts welded around her and refusing to let go.

My friends prepare themselves for their athletic events by emptying a rather impressive number of beer cans, and they fortify their resolve, while performing these athletic feats, by emptying even more beer cans, and when they return to the deck to think back on the amazing athletic feats they have just performed, they empty more beer cans—so by the time Kristen's butt connected with the deck, our friends had thrown themselves into the spirit of her adventure. They awarded her Olympic scores for the fall and its execution. One or two of the more nimble attempted to mimic the stages of her descent. There was a great outpouring of merriment and glee, not all of which was tempered with the sensitivity befitting the occasion.

If you took a poll of fat girls, you would knock on a lot of unfriendly doors before you would find the jolly, fun-loving sport who would answer, "Heck, yes, I love to sit down in a lawn chair that breaks, dumps me on my ass in front of all of my friends, and leaves me there to wonder, *how am I ever going to get back up?*" Kristen would not be one of those women.

She was embarrassed. She was humiliated. She was furious. She managed to roll back onto her feet and then she grabbed the offending corpse and pointed to the faulty welds that had betrayed her. She declared the chair "defective." She planned to go directly to the store where she bought it on the way home and demand her money back. She stood there shaking mutilated sticks of aluminum and plastic weave as if expecting them to reassemble themselves and mumble an apology. For every faltering giggle she heard the rest of the weekend, be it chair-related or not, she asserted that it was not her fault the chair broke, that it was a bad chair, a weak chair, a poorly made and overpriced, cheap chair, and that she would, come hell or high water, exact her revenge on the seller.

Of course this only antagonized the situation. Sometimes good sportsmanship makes you look good and sometimes it just keeps you from looking worse. The urge to imagine this conversation between Kristen and the chair seller inspired friends who had never engaged in imaginary conversations before. The moment she walked out of a room someone would turn to someone else, mug a look of stunned outrage and mutter, "I just sat down in it ONCE and the darned thing BROKE . . ."And everyone would burst out laughing all over again. And because she would not give, not even break a single rueful little grin, the incident has never truly died.

When she bought her house, for her housewarming one of our friends bought her a matched set of oversized lawn chairs. They are very nice chairs. I believe I've even had occasion to sit in one of them.

I did track down the chair-giver and make him sit in it first. Kind of a trial sit. No self-respecting fat girl ever really trusts a lawn chair.

wreck the balls on boughs so jolly

MY MOTHER, MUCH to her own consternation, had five children in twelve years. She found, therefore, great comfort in blanket threats broadcast over a large audience.

It makes little difference what the boys heard or thought of these proclamations because they're boys, and because we girls interpreted everything for them anyway. The UnWee was impervious to threats, unless, of course, they made her angry, which was an immediate call to war. And the Wee One was the blithe spirit of the group, believing that blanket threats either did not apply to her or were just too general to be enforced. I, however, the Least Wee—the oldest child, the rule-keeper of the lot—was a living human sponge, absorbing every rule, every threat, every implied code of conduct as if it were written on stone and handed down to Moses on the Mount. I exhausted much of my childhood trying to live up to these firm, and (I discovered all too late) not always straight-faced edicts.

I never walk on other people's lawns.

I never step on cracks in the sidewalk.

Every Christmas our mother told us that if we were bad, instead of presents we would get a bundle of sticks or a single lump of coal hanging on the back-porch doorknob for Christmas. The UnWee harrumphed it was "not fair," while the Wee One strained to imagine any situation in which she could be considered "bad." I reverted back to midnight of January first of the appointed year and diligently tallied every bad deed I had ever imagined (keeping a separate column for accusations leveled unfairly or not yet proven) and worried. I worried all through November. I worried for twenty-four hours a day for twenty-four days of December. My father, who reveled in torture, would grin at me at odd moments and mutter, "coal, Cheryl," or he would grip the back-porch door-knob, look down at it, and then cock one eye significantly at me. By Christmas Eve I was a basket case of worry and dread, remembering sins of mine too horrid and unforgivable to even be named. Every Christmas morning I ran directly to the back porch and checked for stick bundles before sighing with relief, promising to be better next year, and then dashing to see what Santa had left for me under the tree.

My mother loved Christmas.

She spent hours making fudge and candy and decorated cookies, much of which was immediately packed up in fancy tins and delivered to baby-sitters, neighbors and the people who ran the store down the road. The rest was packed up and hidden in the upper reaches of the cupboards where we were threatened with death itself, should we feel obliged to conduct any more samples. I remember Christmas as weeks and weeks of waiting until we could actually eat the delicacies she made.

She shopped and shopped for the perfect gifts for everyone. She put a great deal of thought into every gift. I remember one year she bought heavy metal Scotch tape dispensers for my father's mother, and my father's mother's mother. They were red, and on the side was a little saying, which was a popular and humorous song at the time—sung on a German accent—*Ve grow*

wreck the balls on boughs so jolly
159

too soon old und too late schmart. My great-grandmother (who had to be in her seventies) was offended because she thought my mother was calling her "old."

It seemed like every night our mother would come sneaking into the house with huge paper bags full of stuff and would tell us not to look. Holding the bags behind her back, she would sneak off into her bedroom. The last week before Christmas there was hardly a door in the house we could open without her swooping down over us like a hyperactive hawk, screeching, *DON'T GO IN THERE . . .*

We bought a tree and put it up and buried it with decorations, and she bristled at the notion of ever using a fake tree when you could fill your house with the scent of pine and the perpetual threat of fire. Year after year my parents got into a fight while testing and retesting and re-retesting the tree lights, and year after year they would end up hugging and smooching in front of the tree when it was finally decorated.

Once the tree was decorated, it was our job, as children, to keep the cats from climbing the tree or batting off the decorations. Virtually every Christmas photograph of our trees, from when we were small, features a cat of varying size, coat or age, either in front of it, behind it, under it or in it. And virtually every Christmas photograph shows a tree with the bottom six inches of branches bare and cat-stripped.

Our Grandmother Molby was a tireless seamstress and a strong believer in properly dressed children, so of course we were measured and stitched and hemmed into new Christmas dresses every year. We celebrated Christmas twice during the day, and so there were always two sets of Christmas pictures of us. Our morning celebratory One-Present-Only opening with just Mom and Dad, where, lined up side by side (often holding dolls), we were dressed in ragged hair and our bottom-back-flap PJs, was one picture. Later in the afternoon, after that interminable wait until the adults had FINALLY washed all of the dinner dishes and we could indulge in our frenzy of greed, once again we were lined up under the tree (often surrounded by massive piles of loot) where we were dressed in painfully exact curls and bows and all of our Christmas finery for photograph number two.

One year the UnWee got a fort set. One year my mother announced that if our father gave her one more small electrical kitchen appliance she was going to find a way to use it on him. One year my Grandfather Molby gave me a desk he had built for me himself. We were neither rich nor poor, but we were wise enough to realize, gradually, that the hunger for things is never fully cured by mere things.

The heart of the celebration was a huge celebratory meal, turkey with all of the trimmings, dressing, mashed potatoes and gravy, green beans, Mother's favorite (a collection of various beans and onions she layered together and allowed to ferment for several days before serving), pickles, olives, candied watermelon rinds, fresh rolls, real butter, milk, candied sweet potatoes, and, as a nice chaser for the fudge, candy and cookies we had been pre-dining on, desserts. More than one dessert.

Christmas was—and is—a time of magic, a time of gathering together in our family. As adults we have retained some traditions and modified others. We have sworn to cut back on the commercialism of the season, while still dashing out to buy this year's trendy equivalent to the Tickle Me Elmo doll ("Christmas," we tell each other solemnly, "is *special*"). Because our generation involves more groups of children and needs to be scheduled around custody arrangements, and because we gather now from farther away, we have switched around the gift-exchange portion of the day. While we still exchange gifts, we exchange fewer gifts at one time, and the ceremony takes up less time than it did when we were children. It is, perhaps, a less important part of the mass family gathering.

The dresses are gone. We girls waffle now between dress slacks and jeans.

A few of us have even gone to fake trees.

None of us dress the bottom foot of the tree, and when someone shows up limping, we automatically know we are seeing the results of a cat-stolen-glass-ball-in-the-foot injury. You learn to take the good with the glass.

the go-get girl

THE YEAR I CAME OUT to myself—*Hi, my name is Cheryl. I think I may be a* (hic) *lesbian*—I went to the Michigan Womyn's Music Festival. I was twenty-seven going on nineteen and one of my friends who had spent her summer listening to me said, "Go to Festival—you might meet some women you can talk to." As luck would have it, that meant she might have a weekend during which she could talk about something else, which would also have been a good thing.

The first year I went to Festival was about 1977. I met a woman who fell in love with me. I had trouble enough loving myself, so I got drunk and fell into a ditch and wallowed a while in the bracken. I remember porta-janes, hauling trash from the kitchen for my workshift, and being horribly, perpetually lost all weekend. I ate non-homogenized peanut butter and bananas (the only food I recognized) and swore I would die before I would strip naked and take a public (cold) shower (although I did watch a few). Alix Dobkin stood on stage and said it wouldn't hurt little boys to learn there are places they can't go either and I thought self-righteously, *I will never become that bitter.* I had a good time, I guess. As usual, I had no sense of history taking place or anything new or radical being forged around me; I was just worried about the nudity. And while I always had the best of plans, I did not go to Festival again for twenty-one years.

My Beloved is a devout Festie-goer, so when I became involved in her life, I found myself packing my sleeping bags and tents and trailing off to into the woods behind her. The Land is different, the food is better, the porta-janes are cleaner and the bananas are just as good. Since I am not twenty-seven anymore and I gave up my job carrying fifty-pound bags up and down a ladder in the factory, I cleverly failed to volunteer for garbage detail as my mandatory workshift this time. Garbage collecting is hard work.

I volunteered for kitchen detail.

Almost everyone does.

The choices are pretty much presented as kitchen detail in the morning, kitchen detail in the afternoon, kitchen detail in the evening or daycare for someone else's kids. The first two years I was given plastic gloves, a sharp knife and a bus box and shown to a huge table laden with never-ending stacks of vegetables.

This year I was promoted to go-get girl.

It seems simple enough. A go-get girl goes and gets. It is a subset of the serving division.

It is at about this point that the fog began to set in.

Before I sign up for my civic duties, I should probably always tell the people around me that I never actually got that little T-shirt in kindergarten that says "Plays Well With Others." I got the one that said "Throws Horrible Tantrums and Sometimes Bites." This is not my fault. I have leadership abilities; everyone has always told me so. My particular skill, all of my life, has been to walk into a situation I know absolutely nothing about and begin organizing everyone around me. (For the record, I dislike this characteristic in nearly everyone else I know. I feel it causes unnecessary conflict. They could just do it my way.) I have no following abilities whatsoever and find them superfluous to my way of life. I should probably also note that I do not always understand the way New Free Lesbians (NFLs) communicate with each other. I have assiduously avoided "processing" for nearly thirty years now. Processing is the method by which six lesbians who fundamentally disagree with each other sit down together and explore in great depth every conceivable nuance of every imaginable interpretation of every feeling any of them have ever had until they come to a workable consensus. They keep telling me it works. It seems time-consuming to me.

So I put on my apron, affixed my nametag and reported to my line. I was assigned to line one. I did not assign myself to line one, some NFL assigned me to line one. She said, as she did so, that she had been wondering where her line one go-get girl had gone, although—as far as I can tell—I had been there all along.

My job, as I understood it, was to go get things my servers were running out of. So I positioned myself to be available for duty and waited for someone to run out of something.

I was standing in my position in line one when another NFL informed me that line three had run out of tomatoes. This confused me because I was assigned to line one, but, ever-helpful, I said, "Okay," and headed toward the food tent for tomatoes.

I was about halfway there when she called me and she said, "You're not from line three, are you?"

I said, "No—I'm from line one."

She said, "I'm sorry—apparently I'm confused—you don't have to go get the tomatoes for line three."

I said, "It's okay—I'm halfway there."

She said, "Still, I'm sorry you had to go all that way for nothing." She appeared to be appeasing me.

I said, "Okay." I went back to line one where my server informed me we were out of tomatoes; however, just as I headed back to the food tent, the go-get girl from line three darted across the lines and delivered a bus box of sliced tomatoes to my line.

This annoyed me, because I could have been going and getting for my own line, if she had paid attention to her line. Instead, she seemed to be dashing all over the place, going and getting for everyone.

I had now walked halfway to the food tent twice and I had gone and gotten exactly nothing. However, I had little time to worry about this because my line ran out of salad. Off I went to the table where the salads are kept, and I acquired one bus box for my line, brought it back, dumped the last of the old salad on top of the new and now I had . . . an empty bus box.

I missed the part of the informational message that would have told me where the empty bus boxes go. This lecture, I presume, occurred when I was right there but missing, just before I was assigned to line one.

So I carried my empty bus box to the beginning of the salad production line and gave it to the lettuce chopper, who took it pleasantly enough, but then frowned and said, "But don't you need a refill?" And she handed me a new bus box full of salad.

I thought to myself, *I will just carry this to line three.* Just as I thought this, the go-get girl from line three zoomed past like the Roadrunner on speed and dashed off again with a bus box of salad.

I estimated about nine people had gone through line one since I had refilled the salad box, so it seemed safe to assume my line was not out of salad yet. So I carried my refill to the table where I got the original salad, set it down, and strode purposefully away as if I were Head Go-Get Girl and no one should question my behavior.

"What else do you need?" I greeted my servers as I returned to my line.

"We couldn't find you, so we sent the go-get girl from line three to go get it," my server replied.

"Lord knows what you'll get," I reflected as the line three go-get girl screeched past, "that womyn has way too much energy for food delivery."

A camper materialized in front of us and set down a small, empty pail and said, "I need this full."

We were informed, as we stood in line getting our serving instructions, that there would be possibly as many as 12,000 womyn at the twenty-fifth Womyn's Music Festival and that many of them—many of them—have issues about food. It was not our job, as servers, to deal with food issues, it was merely our job to issue food. We were, therefore, to serve each camper what we personally considered a "reasonable portion." (Go to the line with fat servers.) If the camper requested more, we were to halve that portion and serve it. If they asked for more, we were to halve it again. If they had questions about the ingredients of the food, we were to direct them to the board in front of the tent that listed all of the ingredients in everything we served. If they had any more complex questions about the food, we were to direct them to the kitchen staff. Very cheerfully our kitchen staff womyn assured us, "We have as many as fifty people we can send them to where they will find out absolutely nothing." We all laughed pleasantly. "However," our kitchen staff womyn assured us, "we have enough food. At no time should you ever tell a womyn, 'No, you can't have more food.'"

So our camper set down her pail, said, "I need this filled."

My server said, "I'm sorry, we're not supposed to do that."

I gasped with shock and horror.

"I'm getting food for several womyn," the camper said. "I need this much food." I could see food issues rising in her eyes: she was ready to fight to death over a small pail of salad right there in the mess tent. No mere server person was going to say "no" to her.

"Well, okay," my server said doubtfully, "but we're not supposed to . . ."

"I'm sure it's fine," I said reassuringly.

She glared at me and half-filled the pail. She waited.

The camper waited.

People began bumping into each other behind her, having expected the line to move ahead by now.

"I have several womyn I'm getting food for," the camper said.

"Just give her the bus box," I suggested, "there's at least one more in the food tent . . ."

"We're not supposed to give them this much food," my server hissed at me and furiously filled the pail. "And besides," she said, looking around, "I'm sure we're out of something . . ."

Of course, in no time we were out of salad. My server pointed this out to me as if it were personally my fault. As if I had dashed down the line when she wasn't looking and told each and every one of the craft womyn coming through line one to tell her they could have more salad than she thought necessary and as a result, once again we were out of salad. I suspect this womyn had been taught to eat what was on her plate and to believe if all 12,000 womyn at Festival had filed through our line, they should have all eaten out of the same salad bus box. I suspected her of having food issues.

I collected the empty bus box and carried it back to the lettuce table for a refill.

The head of the lettuce table looked down at me, frowned—obviously I had gotten something in the wrong order again—but just as she started to speak, the go-get girl from line three roared past with three bus boxes stacked in her arms.

"When you stack them like that, I can only use the top one," the lettuce head said, obviously annoyed.

Apparently not even line three server could do anything right: she was one surly head of lettuce.

"I'msorryIdidn'tknowthat," line three server spit out and flew away with three trays of lettuce.

fat girls and lawn chairs
168

I knew that there would be no point in my walking back to line one with a tray of lettuce—line three server had restocked my salads and was probably halfway to the orchards in California to pick my next box of peaches by now.

I thought bitterly that the line three servers could probably keep all five lunch lines going well into the supper line.

I then thought—utterly without bitterness—that the line three servers could probably keep all five lunch lines going well into the supper line.

I thought, *I have been going and getting for a good hour and a half now and I think I will now go and get my own lunch.*

The lettuce head looked at me and glared, and I said, "We don't need any more, but the server from line three is coming right back," and I laid down my empty bus box and scurried away.

coming out to my father

I FELL IN LOVE with Lawrence Ferlinghetti in the late fall of 1965. I was fifteen and restless to begin my destiny as the Great American Writer; he was a San Francisco Beat poet and my knowledge of him begins and ends with one small volume of poetry, *A Coney Island of the Mind*.

I discovered him in English class. Our assignment had been to find our "favorite" poem and read it dramatically for the class. Being dramatic only by hormonal accident and poetic by much the same route, I trudged along with most of my classmates to the library where we looked under "poetry" until we found something we could read aloud and keep our faces straight and our reputations intact. I may or may not have dug up "Invictus" ("my head is bloody/but unbowed . . ."). In the midst of this heartless adventure in literature, a theater major stood up and read, very dramatically, "I Am Waiting." The class was dumbstruck. This was dangerous stuff. There were ominous thoughts involved in that poem that we were sure we were not supposed to think. I knew I had to own that book.

It was not for sale in Coldwater, Michigan. The nearest bookstore that carried it was The Bookstall in Battle Creek, thirty-five miles away. I advised my mother I needed to make the journey and my mother advised me my father had business there and I should talk to him. When I was fifteen I hated my father and I thought he hated me. (In truth, he hated unbridled emotions, particularly when they were unbridled anywhere near him, but when I was fifteen the difference seemed negligible.) I may have told him I needed the book for class but it seems unlikely because (1) I didn't NEED the book for anything, and (2) I had not yet learned—nor would I for some time—that he would have driven thirty-five miles one way to help me buy a book simply because I said I needed it.

We went in his truck. His truck was pink. It was probably originally red, because I don't remember many pink trucks in vogue in the late fifties, when the Chevy was built, but it had worked hard for a long time and it had faded. The gears were worn so smooth you could shift from first to second without using the clutch, and the body was so rusted that my father carried a riveter under the front seat so that when parts of the body threatened to break loose and fall off, he could rivet them back into place. This seemed to amuse him. He kept his riveter in a cigar box and the rivets themselves were neatly stored in a container just the right size to hold them and to fit into the cigar box, which fit very precisely under the front seat. I could have eaten off the floor of his truck, but he had his little pile of things-he-is-never-without (maps, tools, sunglasses and his portable rock collection) stacked tidily on the seat, so when we reached The Bookstall he had to walk around the truck and open my door for me because the inside latch didn't work. I remember thinking the people inside the bookstore would have been impressed for the wrong reason. I endured a moment of panic that the migrating literati from Coldwater might have beaten me to all the available copies of the book, but soon I had it for my very own, and, drunk with the knowledge that there really was a world out there different—deliciously, exotically DIFFERENT—from Coldwater, and that this very bookstore was not unlike a portal to that great unknown, I turned to find my father scowling at a display case. I assumed he was studying the display and I remarked on the contents (jewelry, I think), but he said, "Why would you do that?"

"What?"

"Why that's just barn-siding."

I explained to him that barn-siding—the gray, grooved, weather-beaten, falling-down siding off gray, grooved, weather-beaten falling-down barns—was all the vogue, that people I knew were actually paneling the insides of their houses with it. He looked at me with baffled disgust and he said, "I could do something like that" (the fact that people would pay money for others to build something that would look homemade was incomprehensible to a man who aspired to make his projects look as professional as possible), and we left the bookstore. He never asked me what the book was about. I never told him because I suspected he would neither understand nor appreciate some Beat poet perpetually waiting for a Rebirth of Freedom and I had some vague sense that I was protecting him from something—that he followed me into the bookstore rather than the other way around, that I was an interpreter for a world where people built new things out of old wood and where words were taken quite seriously.

I have never come out to my father. I am forty-eight and he is seventy. He has changed remarkably, since I was fifteen: he has proven to be a man with a deliciously wry sense of humor, an almost Buddhist acceptance of the whims of fate and fortune, and an occasional aggravation with complications in his life which have, since my mother's death, become my province. As it is his job, as my father, to lend me money and fix my tractors, it is my job, as his oldest daughter, to sort through his life for evidence of unresolved problems, which he stores for me like butterflies in a

glass jar. I rarely actually solve them: more often than not I identify or define them, or tell him what agency deals with problems
like that.

He knows. I know he knows.

We have a covenant of trust, my father and I. I do not present him with emotional, word-intensive problems he cannot
solve. He does not make anti-gay remarks in my presence and
sometimes he has this—mischievous—almost expectant—little
smile on his face when someone else does.

She'll get 'em—she's good with words.

useless information
acquired from men

A NUMBER OF YEARS AGO I was having dinner at a friend's house and we were discussing my interest in photography. I babbled on at length about how my lifetime shot of a deer had been hampered solely by the deer's reluctance to stand still—or even near my camera. My friend's husband smiled and he said, "All you have to do is find out where they sleep and where they feed and settle in somewhere between the two."

I remember smiling at him.

I glanced at my friend.

We both fell over laughing.

At the time I owned (or mortgaged) three-fifths of an acre about a quarter of a mile from the Jackson city limits. No deer slept in my yard. No deer ate there. I'd never seen a deer passing through looking hungry or sleepy. I assumed, at the time, that to follow my friend's husband's advice, I would have to first locate a deer, then figure out where this deer both ate and fed. I might as easily have been fascinated by the hope of shooting wild African elephants.

I may have originally filed this insight under the heading Useless Information Acquired from Men.

He was right.

He seriously overestimated my grasp of the task at hand—but he was right.

A few years after that conversation I was driving down Dalton Road through an area known in that county as Behind the Prison and I was testing out my new 50 × 10 field glasses when I espied several brown lumps on the hillside. I pulled off the road, focused my field glasses and studied . . . eleven sleeping deer. They were deer. They were asleep. I flashed back on my conversation with my friend's husband and I thought:

I KNOW WHERE THEY SLEEP.

They were too far away to photograph and walking around on prison property has never been encouraged by anyone I know, so I let sleeping deer lie.

Perhaps two years ago *Newsweek* magazine carried an article about deer (calling them, among other things, "rats with antlers") and my sister the Wee One read this article and (apparently) memorized it. She and I were driving somewhere one day and I said, "Look—a deer," and she recited everything I now know about this article. Of deer *Newsweek* said, "They're edge-feeders."

We all know that, of course. We are driving down I-94 in the early evening, we glance out the window and there, at the edge of a field, quite near a small wood or at least a hedgerow, is a small herd of deer. They're eating. We are not sufficiently sighted to see deer in the middle of the woods and we almost never see them in the middle of the field—they are always on the edge. Predators are always a factor, but this is also pretty much determined by what they eat—saplings, baby trees, fresh weeds (and as every gardener knows, corn, broccoli, cauliflower, and especially tomatoes. My father has found a tiny rogue herd of specialists who appear to dine solely on tulip blooms). An "edge-feeder" means an animal who feeds primarily on the sort of new growth most easily found on the outside edges of woods. Allegedly—according to *Newsweek*—if you wander into the deep woods the only deer you will find will be either very hungry or very sleepy or perhaps both.

The focus of that article was that deer have adapted remarkably well to coexistence with humankind—in fact, we create exactly the kind of environment where they thrive—and beyond the occasional highway collision, deer seem to be settling in for the long haul with humans, their oddly shod brothers. It appears that of the two, humankind seems to find more objections to this peace and tranquillity than deer do. On the overpopulated, suburbanized East Coast, where one is always on the edge of something, Bambi has lost some of his charm. It must be something he ate.

The more I learned about deer, the more I understood about what my friend's husband had been trying to tell me. They are animals. To find one, you need to know (1) where they shelter and (2) where and what they eat. Once you have narrowed down the basic characteristics of these places, they will be easier and easier to find and—surprise—so will the deer who sleep and feed there.

Unfortunately I was never able to tell him that because I never did know where he ate and my friend kicked him out, so I don't know where he sleeps.

a short treatise on brothers

Oᴜʀ ᴘᴀʀᴇɴᴛs ᴄʀᴇᴀᴛᴇᴅ three beautiful, sensitive, creative children and then, as an afterthought, they had two boys. We were not horribly impressed with their efforts. First of all, the UnWee and I had barely finished raising the Wee One. Whatever else her faults may have been, she never peed us square between the eyes while we were changing her dities. But above all else, no matter what we did to her, the Wee One hardly ever cried. She passed out fairly often—she bled like a sieve at the drop of a hat, and she was forever losing her balance while spinning, or bed-bouncing, or other expressly forbidden activities we had warned her against (*Okay, but remember—if you get hurt doing this Mom is going to spank ALL our butts*). She would more likely purse her little lips and start spluttering in blind rage whenever she felt misused. Our little brother (1) started crying hours after he came home from the hospital and he cried nonstop until he was fifteen. "What on earth have you done to that child now?" our mother would demand, as if we were responsible for his every passing mood.

Nor was he made of particularly sturdy stuff for a child. We tried to teach him to play backlot softball; he wandered across home plate at the wrong time, caught a hearty swing at a pitch, and had to wobble off into the weeds and take a nap. Years later he jumped up to catch a fly ball and slammed nose-to-forehead into a slightly taller boy and broke nine bones in his face. We know how many bones he broke because the doctor X-rayed his head and counted them, and then, conversationally, he asked my mother, "How did he get that fracture to the back of his head?" As usual, our mother failed to appreciate the humor of the situation.

He was a tiny child. For years he was the smallest child in his class and his only escape from terrorization from his classmates was to come home and be terrorized by us. We are probably fortunate he did not join the Neo-Nazis or the NRA. He gradually developed a wicked sense of humor with which he slices and dices all who wander into his sights, but what he did, apparently in sheer self-defense, was grow. When I left for college he was nine years old, seven inches tall and barely cast a shadow: the next time I paid much attention to him he was six feet one inch, built like a football player and there was that whole neighborhood legend about beer parties in the gravel pit behind our house. It can be disconcerting, but it is best never to flinch when you find yourself looking that far up at someone you have deliberately tortured most of his life.

By the time our baby brother (2) came along, we had given up. None of this encouraging old, repetitive skills like learning to walk or talk. We had busy lives by then; we did not have time to stand around and wait for him to learn what the rest of us all knew. We carried him around like a sack of potatoes for years and taught him to point at anything he wanted.

My baby brother (2) was lucky to reach his first birthday, because every now and then he would be left in the care of our father, a wonderful man, but not necessarily the world's best baby-sitter. I particularly remember the afternoon my mother went shopping and left my baby brother napping in his buggy in the dining room. This was the same afternoon my father decided to knock out the wall between the living room and dining room with his trusty sledgehammer. Our baby brother never woke up during all of this pounding, but when he did our mother had to dig him out from under a pile of lath and plaster. I remember our mother said, "What were you thinking?" And our father said "*what . . . ?*" eloquently, I thought.

As a small child he learned to fearlessly toddle out in front of us with his arms up to indicate he wanted our attention. As often as not, I would be riding my bike, and rather than running over him (which always put our mother in a bad mood) I would hang him by the backs of his knees over the handlebars and cradle his body with my arms like the edges of a hammock, and ride him this way around the "P" (shaped) drive for hours. As an adult several thoughts occur to me: the bike that I rode had handbrakes, which I could not reach when he was in my arms; it can be hard to balance a bike with an unpredictable thirty-five-pound weight on the handlebars; the "P" drive was new gravel and therefore hard to navigate and not particularly good landing; I wonder exactly where our mother was. To the best of my recollection, I never did drop him or throw him over the handlebars.

Over time we have all grown into substantial adults. At five feet seven inches I—the oldest—am also the shortest and the widest. The Wee One is five feet ten inches and the UnWee is five feet eleven inches. Our little brother (1) is six feet one inch. Our baby brother (2) is six feet two inches. We are like a human strain of redwood: not only are we tall, we are burly and thick of trunk. To wander slightly off track with the same analogy, a few who have tried to love us have come to admire the thickness of our bark and the steadfastness of our stance, but that is another story. Not many people (besides us) go out of their way to argue with our little brothers. Big Men carry a certain mantle of automatic respect. If nothing else, the Wee One has observed, there is always the danger that one of them will fall on you.

a short treatise on brothers

a meat-lover's biased look at vegetarians

THERE HAS BEEN a rampant outbreak of vegetarianism in the past few years. They have always walked among us, of course, but their numbers are growing and they are fast becoming the Militant Minority that nonsmokers were ten years ago. Years ago, when I was young and occasionally slept on the ground, I was lured to the Michigan Womyn's Festival where, as I wandered like Alice through an amazing Wonderland of semi-naked, self-embracing women, I heard the first trill of vegetarianism:

Oh, YUUUK—the smell of burning flesh . . .

My response was not supportive.

The other day a woman called me out of the blue to tell me she had decided to expand her personal circle of friends and she wanted to include me in it, and would it be possible for us to meet, perhaps for dinner? (I make note of this because it's never happened to me before in my life. Nor, actually, have I ever seized such initiative. I personally am a lay-back-in-the-weeds-and-bat-at-her-ankles sort of flirt.) Where we might eat, precisely, became somewhat problematic, however, because she is a vegetarian relying on a confirmed carnivore to pick her restaurant.

I have nothing against vegetarians except they are hard to eat with. I personally could find everything I have ever wanted to eat at Baskin-Robbins, so of course all of my potential dinner companions except one are nutrition experts. First they gave up fat (flavor) and now they have given up meat (food.) In another year or so I suspect we'll give up going out to eat at all and just wander from cabbage patch to beet bed. And, since I am, in my own way, as devoted to my diet as they are to theirs, I will be forced to pre-eat. I am so well-known for my eating habits that I called in to work sick one day and my desk partner suggested I must have accidentally ingested a lettuce leaf.

From a purely outsider's point of view, vegetarians are a confusing lot. I have vegetarian friends who eat fish. I have vegetarian friends who eschew beef bouillon but who eat chicken. I have vegetarian friends (not many) who become indignant when it becomes clear I do not appreciate the purity of their diet: they do not drink milk, eat cheese, eggs or bird's nests, and only wear the hides of freshly slaughtered polyesters. Like all non-Catholics who are only too aware of the convenience of Catholicism (eat, drink and be merry, for Friday we have only to confess) I tend to sniff at the hypocrisy of vegetarianism without needing to seriously evaluate the philosophy. Being free of contradictory behavior myself, I feel quite comfortable judging my friends.

I have actually gotten into the habit of perusing the menus of new restaurants for vegetarian dishes so I won't be caught breathless in the quest for places to take my friends. I can adapt.

And I understand that accepting a particular discipline that is outside the norm—whatever that discipline may be— requires a certain determined immunity to the many obstacles nonbelievers feel compelled to observe and embrace. It takes guts to buck the system. And I appreciate the camaraderie of kindred spirits.

I also appreciate meat. I was born and raised in the middle of a herd of cows, my horizons broadened by the silhouettes of chicken coops, my senses heightened by the gentle eau de pig. I can appreciate more enlightened attitudes about the right to life of animals, the ecological inefficiencies of a cattle-dependent diet . . . But I like meat. I want it. I crave it. It would take just a bunch of Portobello mushrooms to get me through a meat-free meal with a smile.

It is entirely possible, I suppose, that meat-eaters will eventually go the way of smokers. We will be allowed to eat meat only in special sections of the restaurant. We will have to leave all public buildings and sneak our hot dogs and hamburgers twenty-five feet or more from the front doors. We will no longer be allowed to bolt down Whoppers while riding in someone else's car. Massive lawsuits will be filed against the American Beef Growers Association for primary and secondhand coronary damage done by the deliberate repression of the known side effects of cholesterol.

Anything is possible.

Twenty years ago no one could have convinced me the tide of public opinion could have swung from the occasional malcontent and hyperallergic whiner to a nationwide movement to clean up the air we breathe and the toxins we/those near us stuff into our lungs. I have read, in more than one article, that eventually the human race will learn to eat grains or starve.

I quit smoking. More because I had come to the point (for the third time) when I could either smoke or breathe—but not both—than because it was politically incorrect, but I did quit. I fear, however, you can have my steak when you can pry it from my cold, dead hands.

And, just for the record, regarding all of those cutesy we're-going-to-live-forever-while-being-good-to-the-planet/you're-go-ing-to-keel-over-and-die-horribly-before-your-time remarks that seem to flower among the lovers of vegetables: I'm still not sup-portive. Eat whatever you feel you need to and feel good about it, certainly. But if you don't like what is on my plate, fork it.

# of cats and men

I'VE HAD A BACKACHE, of late. I move much more slowly than I once did. I think about things, like angles and degrees of slant and how to pull on my left sock. My goal in life, for about the last two weeks, has been to avoid unnecessary pain. Everything else goes somewhere behind that.

I inched my way downstairs a few mornings ago to find my housemate and Babycakes having breakfast together at the dining room table. I acquired this housemate because he was in transition between his old house and his new house. He and Babycakes are still becoming friends. Bob was peering through the half-lens of reading glasses at the paper while he steadily spooned cereal out of his bowl. Babycakes, who was spread out across the table top like a fine gold rug, was watching every spoonful go slowly up, sink slowly down, go slowly up, sink slowly down, go slowly up . . .

Being something of a curmudgeon—it's probably the pain—I observed that only one of them was truly supposed to be using the table at a time.

"We've worked this out," my housemate said, and flipped a page of his paper.

And—being racked with pain and attacked by assorted random muscular spasms and contractions—I temporarily forgot exactly what was wrong with that alleged treaty.

In Skinnerian psychology, the flaw is called "successive approximation." (You may quietly applaud. Four years of college and this is pretty much what I remember.) Successive approximation is a term describing the methods by which someone who wishes someone else to do something arranges for that person to actually do that very deed. As an example let us choose as the expectant do-ee, oh, say . . . the cat. The cat—we can call him Babycakes—would like something to be done. To continue our example, we need a doer. Let us just randomly choose, oh, say . . . Bob, my housemate. Babycakes would like Bob to do something for him. We could just recklessly assume this "something" Babycakes would like to have done involves, oh, say . . . food.

Skinnerian psychology is a behavioral philosophy that assumes that for every behavior there is a reward and for every reward there is a behavior. An example springs to mind. A man is eating food. A cat jumps on the table. The cat wants the food. The man has the food. The cat wants the man to give the food to the cat. The man wants to keep his food. The cat must think to himself, "What does this man want, and how would this help me get his food?" The man wants peace. The man wants the cat to sit quietly on the table. The cat says, "Ahhh . . . step one. I have gained the table. I shall reward this man."

The man turns smugly to his housemate and he says, with just a trace of superiority, "We've worked this out." The man has been morally justified. The man has his reward.

The cat smiles. Normally he is not allowed on the table. It is time for step two.

Successive approximation is a slow process by which the doer is rewarded each time his behavior comes closer to being what the doee had in mind than the behavior before it. In this particular example, it will be the cat who will wiggle and twitch his way across the table toward the proposed doer, but the result is the same: the goal behavior is closer with each subtle ripple of fine gold hairs. Thus the treaty—which, in the beginning, was that the cat would sit (on the table, but) on the far side of the table, while the man ate their cereal—has successively approximated its way across the table until the man, the cat, the cereal (and the treaty) are all cozily tucked into one small corner. So closely, in fact, that the cat's nose all but falls into the bowl.

The man is not stupid. He perceives a threat to the peace and tranquillity of his morning breakfast. Gently, firmly, he reprimands the cat. "Your place is on that side of the table," he says, pointing with a milk-laden spoon.

This is the beauty of successive approximation (not to mention cats). The cat does not argue. The cat does not engage in negative social behavior. The cat does not attempt to punish or threaten the man. The cat withdraws. Halfway across the table. He is now not as close as he once was to the goal. He is also not as far away as he started out. He may sing a brief song to convince the man of his sincerity and affection. The cat feels neither, but there is nothing in Skinnerian behavioral psychology that requires absolute or even approximate honesty.

In a previous life I am fairly sure Skinner was a cat.

I studied Skinnerian psychology in the late sixties, just about the time my generation discovered peace, love and the Vietnam War. Good drugs were cheap and all around us. We all wanted to believe that good vibrations and gentle thoughts would change the world, cure greed and patch the hole in the ozone. So we all trooped into 101A psych course, ready to learn how to cure the planet and we immediately learned that (1) Skinner was primarily interested in electrocuting mice and (2) as far as Skinner was concerned, love had nothing to do with it. My, the high moral arguments that erupted from that class. It seems just basic

fat girls and lawn chairs
186

human nature now, the notion that if you reward a child for a behavior the child will probably repeat the behavior, but at the time we had much higher principles. We did not conduct our behavior based on short-term temporal rewards (like fashion, social acceptance, peer pressure or the mores of the time). We were Right. We were Good. We were riding with the angels.

I fought with the amorality of Skinnerian psychology for a long time.

And every day I took that class, the cat I lived with at the time would jump up on my bed, kiss me, sing to me, rub her face against my cheek, then jump off the bed and go sit in the doorway. I would get up, walk down the hall and go into the bathroom, and the cat would come in, wind around my ankles, sit briefly in my lap, sing to me, rub her cheeks against mine, then go sit at the top of the stairs. I would throw on a robe, wander on downstairs, and the cat would run into the kitchen and then back to get me, and then into the kitchen and then back to get me. I would walk into the kitchen and the cat would run up to the cupboard where her food was kept and then to her dish and then up to the cupboard where her food was kept and then to her dish.

Somewhere about mid-term it dawned on me that my cat rewarded me for every behavior that more successively approximated her goal. It was nice that I felt my cat loved me. It was nice that I responded so well to small, furry bodies rubbing against my shins. It was also very nice that I fed her for this. It worked out well for everyone involved.

The problem with Bob's treaty with Babycakes, of course, is that Bob believes what Bob has been led to believe. Bob believes that they understand that when he is finished with his cereal in the morning, Babycakes can have the milk that is left in the bottom of the bowl. There is no guarantee this is the ultimate goal that Babycakes had in mind. It is possible that his twitching across the table oddly like the lion on the Serengeti inching toward a zebra herd merely means that he is anticipating Bob's compliance with their aforementioned agreement. It might also mean he is stalking Bob's breakfast, but far be it from me to interfere with my roommates and their sacred male bonds.

Myself, I have a backache and I am going to go sit on the couch in the sunroom and think calm thoughts about the ozone.

the sad and tragic death
of joey beagle

First of all, what is most important and must be remembered at all times is—I was not there. I may have been in school, polishing my mind, or I may have been pursuing some other wholesome adventure, but you need to know—and remember—that the story I am about to tell you happened when I was somewhere else.

In fact, random people who have known me—members of my family, just as an example—have been quick to point out that various life facts I have presented in the past do not necessarily agree with the fact they themselves remember. My facts are bigger, sometimes. Brighter. Less likely to reflect unfavorably on me. Be that as it may, I leave you, the audience, to evaluate the absolute truth of a story about an incident that happened when—and I may have mentioned this—I was not there.

But first, a brief history of my family.

When we were very young, the UnWee, the Wee One, and I, the Least Wee, were unusually blessed with remnants of preceding generations. I am the oldest, so I can remember not only two grandmothers and two grandfathers, but a great-grandmother (on my father's side), her husband (apparently on no one's side) and a great aunt (on my mother's side). When I was very, very young many of these people were old, certainly, but by my standards today they were not all that old. My father's mother still threw herself belly down on her sled and raced us down hills when I was in my teens. Both of my grandmothers lived into their mid-nineties and my great grandmother lived into her mid-eighties. These people—these women—were around for a long time by anyone's standards.

Apparently because we had all of these living older relatives, the UnWee, the Wee One and I would be seized from our mud pie assembling, face-washed, shod, spit-combed and driven repeatedly to visit aunt- or grand-so-and-so. The world was a much larger place when we were young and our mother did not just recklessly jump into the car and drive eleven miles to the next town for nothing, so I assume there was a good reason for our visits. The evidence would suggest our entertainment was not to be one of them.

In particular, my mother never struck me as being unusually fond of my great grandmother—Gram—nor did Gram seem any fonder of her.

I was partly responsible for this lack of overall goodwill. I laid in the rain.

Obviously this was no great plot on my part; I was only about six months old at the time. I was lying in my buggy and ogling the sun when the sun went away and clouds arose and water started falling out of the sky. Never having been one to cherish discomfort, I'm sure I reported this change to the nearest responsible authority as soon as I became aware of it. The nearest responsible authority came barreling off the porch, intent on saving her first-born from drowning, slipped, fell, and snapped her wrist like a toothpick. She did have the presence of mind to drag me, buggy and all, out of the rain, but immediately after that she had to go to the hospital and have a cast put on her right wrist. My mother was right-handed. Potent family forces determined that she was no longer able to care for a six-month-old as precious as I was with only one wrist—and the weak one at that—and so Gram was dispatched to oversee us.

By all accounts, this arrangement lasted just about a week.

My mother told me Gram was too easily offended.

My grandmother—Gram's daughter and my father's mother—told me my mother was terrible to my great-grandmother and sent her home in tears.

Having listened to evidence presented by both parties, I have determined that you had to be there—which I was, but, as I mentioned, I was six months old at the time and not a particularly good witness.

However, as a result of my unfortunate drenching and my mother's broken wrist and the hurt feelings all around resulting from it, we visited fairly often with Gram, but it was never presumed that any of us would enjoy it.

I should also note that I was an imaginative child. Whenever life became too dull or boring or routine to amuse me, I made up my own reality. I estimate I spent roughly half my childhood writing my own personal novels in the back of my head while ignoring much of what was going on around me. I am a whimsical candidate for the role of family historian.

For a while when I was a child, Gram was married to her third husband, Charles. I was charmed by him because he had had several fingers lopped off in some kind of horrible accident and when he tamped down the tobacco in his pipe, he did it with the stump of his left index finger. I was so intrigued by the sheer efficiency of this action that I suspected if I ever took up the pipe, I too would have my left index finger stumped. Charles Beagle died of a heart attack while walking home from town one day when I was still quite young. For a while he was there and then he was not. I never did know exactly where he went.

the sad and tragic death of joey beagle

I used to like to go to Gram's house because she occasionally made a cocoa/butter/oatmeal cookie called a "no-bake," which I considered to be nature's most perfect food. Actually getting one, however, was tricky. For one, I was raised by my father to lie. I often rode with him on daylong jaunts in his fuel oil delivery truck where I presume I chatted nonstop, a particular skill of mine, while he delivered gas and oil to the farms on his route. I was given strict orders, each time I crawled up into his cab, to tell each and every one of those loving, giving, baking farm women, "No, thank you," when they asked, "Would you like a cookie?" This is the moral equivalent to asking Elizabeth Taylor to say, "No, thank you," when someone offered to give her a diamond—not only was it soundly untrue, it just went against basic nature. Often these farm women would chase me around the back of the truck where they hoped my father wasn't looking and stuff cookies into my innocent pockets for later. Sometimes I felt so sorry for them, driven as they were by their obvious need to feed someone, that I took one. Gram was all the more treacherous, therefore, because not only did she ask you once or twice or three times if you wanted a treat, she seemed to enjoy a perverse form of forced begging.

"Would you like a treat?"

"Oh, no, thank you."

"Are you sure? I know you liked my no-bakes before."

(Quick look at Dad), "Oh, no, that's okay."

"You don't like my treats?"

My dad would bump me. This was one of those father-child signals that had not been fully worked out at that point in our relationship. (Heavy sigh.) "Oh, no, thank you." Had I been Pinocchio, my nose would have been a foot long by now. My mouth was literally watering at the thought of a no-bake.

"Oh, Bob, let the child have something. How about"—she would wink at me and scuttle out to the dining room, and come back triumphantly brandishing the infamous candy dish—"a hard peppermint candy?"

I loathe hard peppermint candies.

I would rather eat peas.

My father would give me his Significant Look now. I could only assume this meant I should continue to lie, so I would sigh and say, "Oh, I'd love one. Thank you very much." And I would take one of the disgusting things and (another particular skill of mine, honed to perfection during pea season) I would do everything a small child can imagine to do with a candy except eat it. When I left Gram's, the insides of my pocket were glued together with little wads of wet, sticky peppermint.

That candy dish has been handed down through generations and a few years ago I nearly had the opportunity to inherit it. I amused myself with fantasies of carrying the dish ceremoniously out to the back porch and smashing it to dust with a rock.

Gram was immensely old, probably in her mid-seventies, and immensely large—as many of the women in my family either are, or struggle righteously not to become—but what my sisters and I remember most about her was her nose. The poor soul was blessed with a huge old Roman nose. We probably would not have noticed quite so much had she not also been a devout and unavoidable snuggler of small children. The moment we arrived she would demand we vault immediately into her lap and begin snuggling and she would burrow that big old Roman nose right into our faces, or our chests, or in the UnWee's case (for the Un-Wee passionately hated snuggling) the small of her back. The thereness of that oversized and witchlike nose was inescapable.

Even worse, her most prized possession was a small parakeet named Joey whom she fussed over as if he were her firstborn. On command the bird would fly to her shoulder, land, walk up and down her arm, and then kiss her on the nose. I may not outlive the observation that his beak and hers were exactly the same shape.

None of us were exceptionally fond of Joey. We had to be careful not to let him out when we came in or when we left. Sudden or loud noises upset him. He begged for food mercilessly (and probably ate most of his meals by her hand) but we were not to feed him. So we would be sitting politely in a chair (we were not allowed to move, at her house), silent as churchmice (we were not allowed to talk, at her house) when the Bratty Blue Baron would fly through and nip a hunk out of our cookie on the way by. He seemed quite aware of the fact that we were to be seen and not heard and he delighted in inciting us into rebellion. One of his favorite forms of amusement was to fly around the house about a foot below the ceiling and strafe small children, dragging his feet through our hair, flying back to Germany or wherever he lived with toesful of our hair as souvenirs. He particularly liked to pester the UnWee, either because she was a strawberry blond, or because she spent most of the time we were at Gram's with her head buried in a paper bag, or under a couch cushion, thus making it more of a challenge for him.

I think it would be fair to say we all hated that bird. I would think that it would be just human instinct, when something flies by at fifty miles an hour and steals your hair, to reach up and smash it.

Apparently, on a day that I wasn't there, the following event occurred. I am quoting my baby sister, the Wee One, and although I will note that she and the UnWee were nearly inseparable as small children and presented a nearly impenetrable front to the outside world, I am in no way suggesting that her story would be anything but utterly true. Our daddy did not raise his little girls to be liars.

The Wee One and the UnWee were innocently standing in a room where the adults were not when Joey flew through, contracted a heart attack in midair, and fell flat on the floor dead.

fat girls and lawn chairs

One minute he was the Bratty Blue Baron: the next he was a cheap pile of used parakeet feathers.

They were themselves astounded at such a sudden change in their fortune. One minute they were being tortured unmercifully by three ounces of flying fuzz and the next, the cursed bird was dead.

I would imagine they just stood there, staring at each other, stunned.

When Gram discovered her beloved Joey dead, however, she was not stunned. According to the Wee One, she carried on like a child of God. She accused the UnWee of budgiecide, she wailed, she cried, she screamed. The woman came completely unraveled.

"She never forgave the UnWee for that," the Wee One has told me, and not a lot of forgiveness has gone on in the Wee One's house, either. "Like we would kill her precious parakeet." And then she informed me the bird fell over dead on the kitchen counter when they were not even in the room.

Myself, I have no idea where or how many times the parakeet died, or how many persons were in the room when it happened because—as I may have mentioned by now—I was not.

the young person's guide for dealing with the impossibly old

I WAS YOUNG ONCE. In fact, everyone I've ever known has made that claim.

I didn't believe them right away. When I was a kid my grandmother used to tell me stories about her life when she was a little girl and I would sit there, gazing solemnly at her silver hair and her wrinkled face and think to myself, "Yeah, right—like you were ever my age." I was a sensitive and compassionate child.

I am now just about the same age my grandmother was when we had those conversations. My hair is mostly silver. I don't have as many wrinkles, but that may be because they're less than three feet away and I can't see them anymore. The backs of my arms are flabby, I am fat, I have rude hairs growing out of my chin and my skin has lost its memory. All of those crude jokes we made about our sixth-grade English teacher have come home. Teenaged boys—once the bane of my existence—now hold doors open for me. The woman who looks back at me from my bathroom mirror is sliding toward her mid-fifties. She'd better be careful—she's getting old.

I myself am about thirty. I've been thirty for about twenty-three years now.

Not much else has changed.

I remember being twenty, but—oddly enough—I'm nowhere near as jealous of twenty-year-olds as I knew old people were when I was twenty. In fact, I am nowhere near as old as fifty-year-old people were when I was twenty. The Important Subjects we all endlessly discussed when we were twenty—birth, death, The Meaning of Life, Why They Don't Just Fix That—all seem sort of . . . done . . . to me now. It's not that I never suffered over them, it's just that some questions answer themselves and others change from one decade to the next. After you've debated the existence of God for thirty years, you understand that no one is likely to change their mind because of any brilliant insight you might give them. Change itself—which seemed so inevitable and necessary when I was twenty—has taken some strange twists and brought on enough unexpected side effects to make me wary these days.

When I was twenty it was painfully important that everyone around me like me and—if not like me—at least understand me. I was a one-woman Peace Corps. Even the opinions of total strangers sitting at adjoining tables mattered. I don't know when that changed. I wasn't paying attention. I am fifty now. I expect the strangers at adjoining tables to mind their own business and I presume I am exactly where I am supposed to be. I no longer assume I am the most interesting person in the room and as I have slowly turned gray I have discovered people don't pay much attention to me anymore. I find that I like this.

An older friend once told my Beloved, "After fifty there is no more bullshit." There will always be bullshit-lovers of any age. But once I hit about fifty I realized that a lot of those dutifully learned rules I've been carrying around—and pretty much ignoring, in my personal life—are just a lot of excess baggage and could probably be dropped along the wayside. It may be a fine-sounding rule, but if I haven't followed it in fifty years, chances of a sudden change now are slim.

the young person's guide for dealing with the impossibly old

My definition of "old" has changed in the past twenty years. When I was a child I decided to die at the age of thirty-six because (1) it would be a long time before I was ever that old and (2) it was obvious there is no point in living any longer than that. This somewhat pre-dated the "die young and leave a good-looking corpse" philosophy of those slightly younger than I am, but it reflects, I believe, our culture's attitudes toward age. (Or, I may have just confused myself with Marilyn Monroe. I could make mistakes like that when I was very young.) Now I see people in their sixties and I ask myself, "Just exactly when do people get old?" Because it's a steadily moving cutoff.

I am happier, more at ease with myself and the world around me, than I have ever been. I am relaxed. I am having a good time—and most of the people my own age that I know are.

Why then, I suppose younger people might ask, do the lot of you seem so cranky? What are the constant references to "young people" like youth itself is some kind of social disease? What is this perpetual antagonism between the young and the older anyway?

I was standing at the counter in a department store with my partner's mother, who was then eighty-two, when I realized that the clerk was talking to me. I wasn't buying anything—my partner's mother was. She knew what she wanted, she had her own money, she was fully capable of making her own decisions—but she is a little hard of hearing. It can make her difficult to talk to. And that simple infirmity, combined with the fact that she is older, has rendered her invisible. The minute the conversation became taxing for the store clerk she turned to me because I was younger. More vibrant. More important. More powerful. Just as we in our fifties begin to realize our parents are really not that much older than we are, we get to watch the world infantilize the old. They become nonpersons. People talk around them or above them instead of to them. They become virtually invisible.

I asked my partner's mother once what it feels like to be eighty-two and she looked blank for a minute and then said, "I don't feel any different than I ever did."

I was hoping for something more profound, but the truth is, I don't either. But I am hoping my mind goes into irretrievable dementia before people start talking to me like I'm three years old again or it's going to get ugly.

the hand that cradles the rock

We HAD GATHERED loosely around a table—siblings and their various entanglements—and we were idly discussing our childhood. Much to the Wee One's chagrin, these discussions almost always go back to the years when she could bleed at will. Often quite dramatically. Her particular specialty was nose-bleeding, but she poured more blood out of her forehead than either the UnWee or I, as well. And in the spirit of a sibling gathering, someone lovingly recalled the time when I hit my kid sister in the head with a rock.

It was an accident.

Actually, given my gift for aim, it was a phenomenal shot.

When we were kids, part of the property my father owned was an abandoned gas station and behind the gas station was a small lot of pure trash. Broken glass, rusty cans, weedling trees and rocks. Lots and lots and lots of rocks. I have no idea why so many rocks had chosen to congregate in one place, but in my father's veins coursed quarts of diluted farmer's blood, and farmers

Hate Rocks.

They hate them.

Leave an old rock in the middle of a road and a farmer will

deliberately drive over it. Back up. Drive over it again. Farmers are death on rocks.

So my father looked out the kitchen window one morning and he saw a herd of rocks gathering in his trash lot and my father said, "We're gonna go pick up those rocks, now." The "we" of this project, of course, were my father and his small troop of slave laborers, the Least Wee (me), the UnWee and the Wee One.

The Wee One was a poor slave. She was (and still is) five years younger than me and a year and a half younger than the UnWee and she used this advantage mercilessly. She was small and cute and wherever she went, we heard the legend, "Why, she looks just like a little Indian." Her face, as a baby, was round, with big brown eyes and straight dark hair, and she tanned effortlessly. In the racially unchallenged community where I grew up, this was enough to qualify someone for the exotic status of "little Indian."

So "we"—two slaves, a slave master and The World's Most Perfect Child—parked our truck in the trash lot, and the slave master got out to talk to my uncle, who had chosen that particular moment to drive by, looking for someone to talk to. The Wee One, feather in hair, opted to stay in the cab. And the slaves—the UnWee and me—were sent to the rock pile. We were ordered to toss the rock pile, one rock at a time, into the back of the truck.

The UnWee and I picked up rocks and threw them into the truckbed, picked up more rocks, threw them as well into the truckbed. Picking up rocks and throwing them into the truck was work.

I was never a strong advocate of work.

I particularly was never a strong advocate of work I was forced to do while others stood idly by, talking, for instance, or perhaps just gazing at their reflections in the cab mirror.

I was feeling righteously abused.

The Wee One sang back from the cab, "I'm gonna come help now."

As if she would have been any help, had she come. She was—give or take—about five. Physically challenged. She couldn't jump three times on a bed without bleeding profusely through the nose, getting us all in trouble, and she couldn't pick up most rocks, much less throw one. She was, I felt at the time, about as close to useless as a kid sister could get.

I thought I told her to stay in the cab. I know I thought to tell her to stay in the cab. Whether or not I actually said it aloud is a question for history.

I picked up a rock, I aimed for the back of the cab, I threw it, and I cold-cocked my baby sister.

Dropped her in her tracks.

I was aiming for the back of the truck, not my sister.

Had I been aiming for the Wee One, I probably would have taken out the back window of the cab, or perhaps the windshield of one of the passing cars behind me. I know, in my heart, that I did not deliberately throw a rock at my sister because I have never actually hit anything I aimed for.

She stumbled around in circles about three times, reached up to touch her little Indian head, wiped away a fistful of blood, and my father swooped her up in his arms and whisked her off into the house.

This is the end of my memory tape. Nosing about for more, I find no traces of remorse and not a great deal of regret. I was aware that my father was angry about the incident, but not aware that he was angry with me. I was shocked and astonished to learn, some forty years later, that various members of my family either believed or at least entertained the belief that I committed that heinous act on purpose. That I intended actual physical harm to my beloved baby sister.

I did not.

fat girls and lawn chairs

I would not have been profoundly disappointed if great bodily harm had come to her, but I certainly was not going to volunteer. She bled most of the time and it almost always came to be my fault. She was small and delicate, it was explained to me, and apparently had the common sense of a goose: I was older and stronger and smarter and more responsible. It was my job, therefore, to keep her alive until her brain began to develop. I don't recall, just offhand, what I ever did to deserve such a thankless job.

Ironically, after I beaned her in the skull with a small rock, I was reprimanded—but it was still my job to keep her alive. Eventually our mother took her to the doctor and had the inside of her nose cauterized so she didn't leak so much, and no longer suffering from blood loss, her brain did begin to work. Once utterly useless, she now cooks and sews—she sews and appliqués and quilts beautiful, creative wall-hangings and other fiber arts—she mothers my nephews and my niece and she is even interesting to talk to. In fact, as an adult, she is one of my favorite people. Today, I still can't throw a rock and hit what I aim for. But if anyone hit her in the head with a rock, I would be forced to drive over to their house, corner them in their back yard, and beat them mercilessly with my own rock because she is my baby sister, and it is my job to protect her.

does a bear . . . ?

THOSE OF US with crippling disabilities lie always cautiously on the edge of polite society, waiting for the next challenge. For instance, last weekend in the middle of a Solstice Celebration, our hostess—a kind and supportive friend—asked us, her guests, to help her defend her faltering garden from marauding deer by peeing its perimeter. Sadly, there are those of us who would, unfortunately, burst like fine, overheated melons before our cast-off fluids will dampen the greens. This is the painful disability I have lived with all of my life—if there is no porcelain bowl involved, the need may not diminish but the deed will go undone. I cannot pee in the woods.

Or on the lawn, or in the garden, or in the back forty of somebody's field.

I can bare my butt with the best of them, I can crouch—sort of—and neatly remove my pants from the line of fire—or water—but there's really no point.

In fact, I can be squirming uneasily across the lawn to certain porta-janes, walk inside, and the whole sense of urgency can vanish in a flash. *Nope*, my body says firmly, *we will be making no contributions here*.

My friend and hostess had only recently completed a several-week trek down the Appalachian Trail and so I presume peeing in the woods now comes quite naturally to her. It made sense to her that her friends, with all of their needs and all of their inherently human smells, might wander over to the garden and cop a squat rather than walk all the way to the house and contribute to the disposal problems of the city. The garden-eating deer would be offended and go elsewhere for their salads, our friends would be returning their essence to nature, and the passing train engineers might get a glimpse of something to brighten a dull day. Under the circumstances, it would seem almost bad guestmanship to decline. Still, however willing my spirit may be, my bladder won't budge.

I have no idea why I am pee-impaired. Perhaps it is a reflection of my birth order, that having been the oldest child of a family of five children, I absorbed the rules of social discourse not once, but five times, and am, therefore, excessively socialized. My two-year-old nephew, patterning diligently after his father, often stood on the edge of his parents' property and stared intently off across the cornfield with one hand coiled—empty—in front of his fly. He had determined that this is something that men do, even if the purpose of the ritual eluded him. I, on the other hand, patterned after my mother, who seemed obsessed with the notion that all cast-off fluids be disposed of in the white bowl in the bathroom. In fact, she was known for her fairly dramatic efforts to drag offenders to the proper shrine even as they leaked and dribbled along the way.

All of my life I have made an honest man of Freud. I admit it—I have envied the penis. Its sexual skills never impressed me much, but I have always appreciated the efficiency of the hose. My own goddess of bodily emissions is rather unhandily buried and not particularly receptive to direction. On those rare occasions when I have successfully squatted in the woods and persuaded a healthy flow, the flow flowed either down my leg or directly into my wadded-up pants. I once filled my left shoe. These experiences have probably led me to a psychological fear of failure. All those years of envy have brought on my own unique brand of impotence. And now—way too late in the game for it to matter—a male friend of mine has admitted that his hose is no more predictable than mine and he too squats to pee.

And there is always the dubious okay-ness of wilderness peeing. Several years ago some friends and I were canoeing down a northern river and we stopped somewhere in the woods to relieve the copious supplies of beer my friends had been consuming. "Oh, it's easy," my friend assured me, "just grab the edge of your suit and shove it to one side." I wanted to go along and watch this feat of agility and engineering, but it seemed somehow unacceptable. It is fortunate I didn't go with her, because minutes later she came vaulting through the weeds like a deer shouting, "Go . . . go . . . get Going . . ." It seems she had squatted, pulled her suit to one side, and begun relieving herself of used beer when she glanced up and discovered, not more wilderness, but the back porch of a riverside cottage and an irate cottage-owner stalking over to demand what she was doing. We all leapt into our canoes and beat a hasty retreat downstream while the enraged cottage-owner stood on the bank and shouted, "How would YOU feel if people came to pee in YOUR back yard?!!!"

The whole incident just sort of dampened that whole together-in-nature feeling.

watching cranes

IT WAS A cold and blustery November day, colder than it had been, but not as cold as it was going to be. The sky was gray. The trees, which had clung stubbornly to their leaves that fall, had suddenly thrown them all off—some still green—so that the trunks wore ground skirts of wilted gray-green leaves, thick and in nearly perfect circles as if they all dropped straight down. Everything was changing, making rushed and ill-prepared concessions to winter. In the ditches alongside the roads wildflowers chilled on their stalks as if they had expected either more warning or more time.

There is something in that weather, which I can feel but I can't describe, but it whispers to sandhill cranes, "go—*fly.*" Once purely by luck I stood on the edge of a stubbled cornfield and watched several hundred cranes dance to each other, call back and forth to each other, jump into flight and rise up into the crisp November air as if they were being sucked into the sky by invisible tornadoes, still calling down to their flock mates as they spiraled up into the thermals. I had no idea what I was watching until I read about their migration rituals later in a book. But I saw it. And I remember the air. Crisp. Sharp. Something changing.

We chose that particular day to drive to Jasper Pulaski State Fish and Wildlife Area in Indiana to watch the cranes stage. None of us had been there, but when I was single I made the transition from fall to winter every year chasing cranes, and now that I am with my Beloved I try to drag her to at least one crane watch every fall. Our friend Rae is addicted to loving anything that won't love her, so of course the cranes fascinate her, and to finish the foursome we invited my dad. I hadn't seen much of my dad that summer or fall. I'd even managed to miss the annual fishing trip on his boat on Lake Michigan, and I was beginning to feel like the prodigal daughter.

I love my father. I sometimes miss the all-seeing, all-knowing, all-powerful mangod of our childhood, the one we were all destined to stand before as soon as he came home: but the woman who created him is gone, and the magic left with the magician. The man she left naked and unprotected in her leaving is a kind man, a gentle, caring man who does not pry and tries not to judge. There is something childlike about him that fascinates and amazes me. He has the power to see mystery in ants, art in the stones in a river. He carries with him always a certain sadness or guilt that he was not the father we should have had. Perhaps all parents carry that. I could have been a better daughter, myself. I could have paid some small attention to the man who had always been there before I reached my mid-twenties and my mother got sick and fell, pulling down the elaborate curtain she had built around him. Sometime during his life he could have learned to talk. But I am the daughter that I am and he is the father he is. The silence will hold an infinite number of the things that we could have said.

I have taken him on crane watches before, but he never even asked why we were leaving for a dusk event at ten o'clock in the morning. We left early because, first of all, we needed to eat breakfast. We stopped in Constantine at a little diner Rae knew about. Somewhere in Rae's past there is a restaurant, The Mother Restaurant, some seminal experience in dining. She has eaten at least once in every restaurant in the three nearest counties, she's the first to know when they rise up and the first to know when they fall, she knows who owns them, who runs them, who works there, and—of course—if the food is any good. Myself, I like to eat, but it goes beyond the food for Rae. She is also a truly good cook in her own right. I just follow her around, eating where she tells me to eat. I've only had one bad meal eating with Rae and it took over a year to get the ban lifted on that place. Don't feed Rae a bad rib tip.

As we were walking back to the car my dad said, "I used to fish in that dam." This apparently happened when he was a kid.

"What did you catch?" I asked, but he shrugged. "Do you want to go down and look at the water?" I pursued. We have a long history of walking down to look at the water.

"Na," he said, and got into the car.

Who took you fishing in Constantine? Did you have fun? Did you spend all day, or were you on the way somewhere, or . . . ? Sometimes he seems so alone that I want to connect him with someone. If not me, then someone in his past. Someone. I never know if he is lonely or if that is just how I see him. But somewhere I learned to stop asking my father an endless series of questions—probably for the wrong reasons now, a lesson too well learned and habitually misapplied. I "talked too much" as a child. Sometimes my heart tells me my father talked too much when he was a child. I learned to ignore that message, to go away in my head and write stories for a more appreciative audience. My father learned to stop talking. And perhaps that's not true at all. I think it is. I think my father paid dearly to become the man his parents wanted him to be. But he did it. My father has always done what was expected of him.

Perhaps I feel perpetual guilt around my father because I did not become the daughter he wanted me to be. I don't even know what he wanted me to be. Probably not a lesbian. I'm guessing not a writer who twists his life to her own point of view and displays it like a movie on a theater wall for all of her friends to see. I could have grown up, married a decent man, had a couple of kids and quit pushing him into experiences he never imagined would touch his life. Perhaps he doesn't feel that way at all. When we were kids, our whole family went over to his parents' farm almost every weekend. After his father died, our family—and his sisters' families—had breakfast with Grandma nearly every Sunday morning. This outing to see the cranes is the first breakfast he and I have had together in over six months.

But first we took him shopping.

The Jasper Pulaski State Fish and Wildlife Area is about forty miles south of Michigan City, Indiana. Michigan City may be famous for any number of reasons, but the people I know go there to shop at the outlet mall or gamble on the floating casino. It used to be that the boat actually left the dock and floated out onto Lake Michigan, but it docked permanently a few years ago. As soon as Rae realized we were going anywhere near Michigan City she made plans to stop at the outlet mall and replenish her jeans. She needs four pairs of jeans to live comfortably: wear and tear had taken her favorites and wounded another pair.

My father does not shop. He's a good sport—he would probably do anything we suggested, maintaining a pleasant demeanor as long as he possibly could—but I could tell by watching him that spending a day buying damaged or outdated goods was something of a mystery to him. The last I knew he bought his jeans at a truck stop because he stopped there to eat and the jeans were on the rack on the way out. He followed us around the mall and eventually bought a CD by Faith Hill, which is more than he buys on most shopping trips.

Then—since we were there and since we still had some time to kill before we needed to get to the park—we went to the gambling boat. My Beloved, suspecting he had never been gambling, thought it would be an adventure for him.

On our way to the boat, however, we took a wrong turn and wound up in the marina, which let us discover the pier and the beach. In November the only takers at the volleyball nets were teams of seagulls. Angry white-capped waves rolled up to take the shore. Still, part of my father will always be in the winds over Lake Michigan. I sensed him grow taller, stronger as he and I ambled down the beach. We both pulled out cameras and vied for shots of the lighthouse. Impossible shots from too far away, to match a hundred more old lighthouse shots buried in drawers at home, but we are water people. Displayed prominently on his wall at home, nestled in among posed shots of his children, is the photograph I took of his favorite fishing spot, buoy #2 in Tawas Bay, Lake Huron. It has never seemed odd to any of us to share our wall of honor with a buoy.

This love of water, however, does not necessarily extend to floating gambling.

I believe my father is the founder and true believer of the Too Good to Be True Club. I remember as a kid excitedly showing him that we had just won a $1,000,000 from Publishers Clearing House—all we had to do was send a card back and we would be rich. It became immediately clear to me that my father did not believe we even deserved to get something for nothing, much less that we were likely to soon. The con artists who prey on the elderly would have their work cut out for them, trying to part my father from his money. As we walked into the jangling cacophony of the riverboat he stayed close enough to my elbow to all but touch me. I could see his eyes traveling the room, a stranger on the wrong planet, surrounded by people who deliberately risked losing money for entertainment. I didn't even try to get him to gamble his own money, but I thought if I put mine in, he might play for a while. We started with the dollar machines, but I realized almost immediately that I was never going to be able to keep my father actively throwing good money after bad for an hour, so we traded down to quarter machines and then to nickel machines. I gave him a wad of change and he gambled until he lost it. But then he wasn't interested in losing any more of my money and he certainly wasn't going to waste his own.

I hunted up my friends and advised them we had exhausted this entertainment adventure. I still had three one-dollar tokens in my hand, so instead of cashing them in I figured I might as well gamble them away. This turned out to be problematic because— when I made it down to the last one—that one won five more, and a few spins later I had fifteen one-dollar tokens.

I thought to myself, "You know—at this rate. . . ."

But I am my father's daughter, and I don't believe I'll ever make my fortune gambling on a riverboat, however tempting the dream may be. I cashed out.

The Jasper Pulaski State Fish and Wildlife Area is in the center of what was once the Kankakee Marsh. Over a million acres of wetlands. Around the turn of the century, mankind, in our infinite wisdom, drained it and turned into farmland. I know almost nothing about the area except that it is the largest staging area for migrating sandhill cranes east of the Mississippi River. I was more familiar with the Phyllis Haehnle Sanctuary in Jackson County, Michigan, and the nearby Baker Sanctuary in Calhoun County. Haehnle is the largest staging area in Michigan. It is the first place where I watched cranes fly in from the fields in the evening. A large wetland all but inaccessible to human beings, it can be seen from the side of a hill about half a mile from the cranes themselves. When the weather is just right and there aren't many people around, you can sit on the bench on the hill at Haehnle and four or five cranes will fly in about twelve feet over your head. You can hear the wind in their wings. This is as close as I have ever come to experiencing true spirituality.

Whenever I talked to veteran birders about Haehnle, they would say, "You have to go to Jasper Pulaski."

Haehnle is a sanctuary owned by Audubon and it caters to preservationists: Jasper Pulaski feels more like a hunting camp. Visitors are reminded more than once that the fine viewing tower, as well as the land itself, was built and is maintained through revenue from sportsmen. One senses the controversy over killing for sport is never far from the surface at Jasper Pulaski.

The viewing area is a huge tower where visitors can stand to look over several hundred acres of green field. We arrived in the late afternoon. We had seen perhaps eleven cranes feeding in the fields on the way to the wildlife area and I was beginning to feel depressed. We had spent the whole day trying to get there, and there was not much to suggest that any cranes were anywhere near us. When we got there, there were perhaps a hundred cranes standing at the very back of the field, near what appeared to be a ditch or what my people would call a "crick."

Not that far from the viewing tower there was one juvenile crane, all alone. The same conversation floated along the tower from one group of people to the next. *He's been there all day—he never went out to the field . . . He's probably sick . . . I wonder where his parents are . . . I wonder what's wrong with him? I wonder if his parents will come back for him . . . ?*

Overhead a string of about eleven cranes flew in, dropped their feet, arched their wings, and floated to the ground like milkweed seeds.

As the sun began to set its residual warmth began to fade with the light. Ribbons of cranes appeared over the treetops and drifted in from the east, the north, the west and the south.

Sometimes as many as two or three hundred cranes would be visible in the sky at once, strung along in groups of two to fifty, all headed for the field. Their call, prehistoric and resonating, cut through the air. The cranes on the ground would call back, as if they were schoolchildren calling to their friends, and more cranes appeared over the horizon . . .

As more and more cranes flew in, the juvenile would peep to them, as if looking for his parents. Occasionally a group would land not far away from him, stalking Egyptian-like over to check him out, but then they would eventually stalk away . . . He should have been feeding, storing up energy to trip. Within days his companions would leave for Florida, flying as much as five hundred miles a day, and he would have to be able to keep up or he would perish. The green field stretched out ahead of me steadily filled in with sandhills until it became a sea of gray.

I have never been completely at ease with nature. I understand that if each infant survived the planet would be neck-deep in grasshoppers the first summer. I understand that the strong survive and the weak perish for the good of the species. I understand that the survival of the whole is infinitely more important than the fate of one individual. Still, the randomness of it all disturbs me. Like car-shattered deer on the side of the highway, there are reminders everywhere that this immensely complex and beautiful web of life that surrounds us is utterly indifferent to the fate of any single individual in it. Like the sick juvenile crane, they become absorbed in the flock around them. I lost him eventually, and when I worried about him to my Beloved she said, "Oh, I saw his parents fly in and beak him around the ears and he went off with them—he's fine." But will he be strong enough to fly?

Surrounded by birds gliding through the sky I turned to my dad. "Do you like it?" I checked.

And he grinned. Some things he doesn't need words for.

Cranes have been staging in the fall in the Midwest far longer than my people have wandered down to watch them. Evidence suggests they have always held some mystical fascination for us: prehistoric man carried crane bones around in his medicine bags. Something about that apparently effortless flight, the aloof indifference to us—the steadfast determination to live as far away from human beings as possible—intrigues us. Standing on a tower next to a field and looking up at a sky filled with incoming cranes makes my heart swell. I feel I am touched by history.

As dark fell we walked back to the car and drove home. It was late by the time we got to my house: I checked with my father to see if he was okay to drive the additional hour home, but he assured me he was. I hugged him. He left.

He never mentioned the double vision. Three days later he went to his optometrist, who told him it was not a vision-related problem and he should consult his regular doctor. Within the next week and a half he would have as many as three more strokes, which ultimately blew out the vision in the right side of both eyes and damaged his short-term memory, and he developed some frustrating aphasia for a man who has never talked very much anyway.

As promised, the weather keeps getting colder.

tinker

My FIRST CLEAR MEMORY of my father is specific, as crisp and immediate as a photograph. I am standing on the burned-out foundation of the garage where he parked his truck and I am looking eye-to-eye at his back tire. He is not there.

He drove a fuel oil delivery truck. Before that—during my lifetime—he tested milk, but apparently he managed this without my supervision. I remember his red-and-white bulk oil truck. I remember hurrying out to the foundation with him each morning and huffing along behind him as he completed his ritual inspection of his rig. His truck is the first solid object I remember appreciating for its size, its density, its irrefutable properties of depth and dimension. I was shorter than the tires. I banged my head walking under the corner of the back bumper. My father was six feet tall and he was in his early twenties when I was a toddler and he walked fast. I went everywhere we went at a dead run. And at each corner of his truck I would find myself scowling at his tire, which was taller than I was, alone, unprotected, utterly abandoned by the one person in the world I wished to be with.

I was annoyed with him. He was not paying adequate attention to my needs. I was my father's firstborn, but I was not his oldest child. Before I came along to destroy the peaceful symmetry of their lives, my parents had lived quietly with their beloved dog, Tinker. I remember Tinker remarkably well for my age at the time. He had long, silky black-and-white hair that stuck to my fingers for no apparent reason. He had a row of tiny little teeth flanked on each side by great white fangs which spent an inordinate amount of time pushed right up in my face. His chest was three feet wide and rumbled continuously. I never saw my own fingers, when I was a child, because he was always nipping at them and I learned to walk by grabbing his coat and hanging on for dear life while he towed me down the road and tried to sell me to every passing stranger he could find. There was no love lost between Tinker and me. He hated me, and since my parents (apparently) wouldn't let him eat me, he devoted his short life to standing staunchly, resolutely, I'll-die-before-I'll-lose-to-the-likes-of-you determinedly between me and anywhere I wanted to be. When my parents were watching, he guarded me as if I were crusted with the crown jewels.

My mother used to tell me Tinker rode around on the floorboard on the passenger side of our car and whenever she braked too quickly, I would tumble off the seat and land on him. For her, this story demonstrated his devotion to me. Once when she was downtown stopped at a traffic light, two men walked up to her car, one opened her door and one opened mine, and they started to slide in and take us away. Tinker (cowering as he was on the floorboards, trying to duck small, flying children) had apparently had a bad day and those men were the last straw and as he jumped up and expressed his aggravation with the whole situation, both men slid right back out of the car and ran on down the street. "Tinker was very protective of you," my mother would tell me.

The thing he took the greatest delight in protecting me from was the company of my father.

I am standing at the corner of my father's truck. I am looking straight into the back tire, which is taller than I am. I used to be walking with my father, but my father has turned the corner and now I am alone.

Almost.

I can hear the triumph in his little dog laugh. I can smell the gloat in his thick, hot dog breath as he flashes those little teeth at my fingers like a disembodied set of clicking jaws, fluttering, snapping everywhere my fingers go to get away from him as he backs me, one angry, frustrated step after another up against the garage wall where I am blocked, the wall behind me, the dog pressed up against me, growling, reminding me that our souls will meet and spar forever on the far side of the coals of Hell . . .

I have no recollection of ever being bitten.

He knocked me down. He stood on me. He dragged me out to the Suzy House and taught my father's goat (Suzy) how to knock me over and stand on my shoulder straps so I couldn't get up, but that is, perhaps, a different story . . . I have no memory of how my parents came to understand Tinker and I were not friends. I was terrified of dogs for years after my parents finally found him another home and perhaps I was honestly terrified of him. What I remember is being pissed. He tormented me. He was bigger, faster, meaner—a rogue shepherd. Some mutt combination of a border collie and the gatepost, he dedicated every herding instinct he had to making my life miserable.

And my guess would be that I never did a single thing to make that dog resent me. My motives were pure. My conscience is clear.

To this day I can still feel my little fists just buried in all that soft and silky hair.

making jam

Lᴀsᴛ Sᴇᴘᴛᴇᴍʙᴇʀ my father became gravely ill. In October his girlfriend retired early to take him home and care for him, in November he had two valves in his heart replaced, and in December she flew to Alabama to buy a house. My father lives in Michigan. My father has always lived in Michigan. In seventy-six years my father has drifted exactly eleven miles from the farm where he was born. I can only assume she decided that he wasn't going to drift any farther and if she wanted to move back "home" it was time to go. That, or taking care of my father can be overrated. The summer she left she had her right knee rebuilt, and her sisters—all of whom live conveniently in Alabama—gathered together to make jam.

I know this because the following spring I went down to fetch my father who had drifted to Alabama, and she gave me two jars of jam and told me the story of how they were made. Her two sisters told her to rest her healing knee on a footstool and there she sat, doing what she could, while they fluttered around her and did everything else, and when they were all done, they gave every third jar of jam to her. I can see this woman sitting quietly on a stool while other women worked around her—I'm suspicious they piled the jars in her lap and made her hold her share, just to keep her down.

I remember my mother canning tomatoes. She once did something to several quarts of concord grapes and every hot summer after that another jar would explode in the basement. We never ate them—they looked like jars of purple eyeballs to us. (We used to add grapes to our mud pies for exactly that reason.) She made strawberry and raspberry jam. In the beginning I think she put up corn and froze green beans and peas, but corn developed a reputation for killing people if it wasn't done right and she lost confidence. We were not really a green beans and peas sort of family and I think she lost interest in working that hard to preserve food none of her children would eat. We lived on tomato products. We ate goulash and chili and tomato soup and homemade pizza and Spanish rice and meatloaf. We ate so many tomatoes in my family that I developed a passionate craving for white sauce that haunts me to this day. I remember being drafted as a tomato-picker or strawberry-huller or pea-shucker, but if my mother's sister ever came over to help us I don't remember it. And it's possible that my grandmother came over to supervise us as well, but again, I don't remember it. I remember my mother alone in the kitchen, where she directed little puffs of air at the bangs that fell in her eyes while she scalded an endless supply of large glass jars. In our family putting up food was a solitary sport.

Eventually I moved out of my mother's house into an apartment of my own, where I immediately noticed a critical shortage of food. Not only was there no store food—there was no "free" food, like homemade jam or canned meat or frozen peas. In my mother's house I could have survived that sort of deficit for months on end, relying on canned tomatoes alone for sustenance. My new independent apartment was a dismal disappointment. A disappointment nearly as crushing as the day I took my

fat girls and lawn chairs
220

spanking new paycheck to a grocery store and compared it to the price of store-bought jam. It's possible the first grocery item I ever bought was a jelling substance to distinguish my homemade jam from ice cream sauce.

What made making jam particularly appealing to me, that first year—that is, after I recovered from sticker shock after pricing a pint (not a quart, a pint) of black raspberries in the produce section—was the realization that I knew where to get them for free. I went immediately to my father's garden, only to discover he had vanquished his mortal enemy, the black-shelled pesky berry beetle, by tearing every berrylike bush, shrub and plant out of his garden. He doused them with gasoline. And then he shot at the escaping beetles with his twelve-gauge as they tried to fly away. He is not a violent man, but he takes his gardening very seriously. This was not a horrible setback to my independence: black raspberries grew wild in the gravel pit, and they were mine for the picking. They could have benefited from my father's benevolent pruning. It was a pain to dress like I was going to a mosque on the hottest day of the year, just to keep my flesh intact. I resented the chiggers for weeks after that. But within perhaps two hours I had enough black raspberries to keep myself in jam all year.

I had never actually made black raspberry jam before, nor had I ever watched anyone else do it. I was not terribly clear on the difference between jam and jelly. Fresh out of college, perpetually strapped for cash, I could have used a little dental work that I could ill afford. I made a substantial batch of jam to see me through the cold, hard winter, but it lasted considerably longer than that because raspberry seeds are plentiful (one might almost suspect they are the point) and they are small only until they get wet. Nothing will locate a cavity in a back molar quite like a swelling raspberry seed. The following year I did a little more research on how to avoid being chigger-bit, and I learned how to make seedless raspberry jam. And then I moved farther from home and therefore farther from easy access to free raspberries, and I never made it again.

Many, many years went by.

I met my Beloved.

I said, "I don't cook."

My Beloved cooks for relaxation. My Beloved cooks for emotional gratification. My Beloved cooks because she's good at it and people admire her for her cooking skills. All of this positive reinforcement incites her to invite great herds of people to her house or public parks or even more exotic arenas where she can display her cooking skills. When my Beloved is bored or irritated with her day job, she turns to our friend Rae and says, "Let's open a restaurant." Watch my Beloved's partner jump for joy at the idea of waiting on people for a living. Keep watching.

The year before last my Beloved, our friend Rae and I jumped into a car and toured southwestern Michigan, looking for inexpensive black raspberries. We learned that there is no such thing. First of all, not all that many people grow black raspberries. (I suspect the cost of all those twelve-gauge shells is prohibitive.) Those who do are apparently former diamond-miners trying to recoup their losses. I believe we may have paid about a dollar a berry that year—seeds and all—and once we'd removed the seeds we had this minuscule little supply that made my Beloved's habit of giving away small jars of jam to people who just happened to wander into her house something of a heartstopper. Black raspberry is my personal all-time favorite jam.

Last year I said, "Raspberries grow wild over half of southern Michigan—let's forage." And forage we did. Up and down roadsides, out behind the cemetery, we spotted every unguarded, unwanted, untended raspberry patch in three counties and we picked and we bled and we waded and stumbled and met more wildlife on a cooking expedition than I've met on most wilderness hikes. We brought our booty home, washed them, crushed them, de-seeded them, jammed them . . . We had black raspberry jam right up through mid-December. It takes a heap of pickin' to make a batch of jam.

In fact, we spent most of last summer preserving things. We made strawberry jam, peach jam, raspberry jam and plum jam. We made pickled beets and three kinds of pickled pickles (one dill and two sweet). We stuffed peppers, we canned tomatoes, and made two kinds of salsa (mild and hot). We made sweet pepper rings. (This is, of course, the use of the royal "We." I personally washed things and cut up things and shouted encouragement from my stool. I'm in training to have my knees redone.)

This year I thought, "I'm lobbying for more black raspberry jam." But since I am the weakest link, I could lobby quietly without drawing undue attention to myself simply by picking more berries. I thought I was prepared.

Echoing across the state line, plaintively, like the cries of a lost child, came the legend: "I want to make jam with you this year."

My Beloved's girlchild—Our Daughter—is a wonderful woman and I love her dearly, but she is six feet of red-headed ambition and meeting her for the first time is not unlike walking into a set of spinning airplane propellers. Like her mother, she radiates energy. Her entire body emits a low hum reminiscent of power lines and those of us who are less innately driven have a tendency to wander off after some shared time and take a little restorative nap. The two of them together can shift a simple little jam-making project into a one-day campaign to save entire continents of children from starvation. The two of them together fondle the word "compulsive" as if it were their firstborn child.

At the onset of my Beloved's jam-making project, therefore, we had our usual crew—my Beloved, Rae and me—my Beloved's mother (Big Momma), a spare granddaughter, my

Beloved's girlchild, her partner, and the girlchild's exhausted baseball-playing son all gathered to make jam. Since the kitchen is not all that large, it only made sense to send the shortest generation into the conservatory to watch videos. The girlchild's partner and I declared ourselves survivors of previous energy bursts and moved ourselves to areas least likely to be sprayed by stray fire.

Big Momma was sent to the market to purchase the berries (straw). There had been some discussion between the dispatched and the dispatcher concerning exactly how many berries might be needed, but Big Momma did some recalculations while she was shopping and she returned to the home front with twenty-four quarts of strawberries. This was deemed insufficient and she was dispatched again. This time she returned with two more cases of strawberries, giving us a total of forty quarts. We needed a few left over, she explained, for our shortcake.

We hulled forty quarts of strawberries.

We had enough five-pound bags of sugar to stop a small flood. Rae and the girlchild's partner took turns doling out sugar in seven-cup increments while the girlchild ran forty quarts of strawberries through the food processor, and then Big Momma gave stirring lessons to all who hoped to achieve the high honor of becoming a Pot Mistress. We dragged out three dozen big pots because otherwise we would still have had counter space left in the kitchen. We were ready to begin.

One batch of strawberry jam: bring five cups of mashed berries and one box of jelling substance slowly to a boil. When the berries reach a full rolling boil (this is a technical cooking term, by the way, "full rolling boil"), have Big Momma solemnly approve a precise measurement of butter to be added to the pot (to reduce "foam"). Only Big Momma can recognize the exact amount. Add seven cups of sugar, stirring constantly, and boil for one minute. Remove the pot from the stove, skim off the foam, and quickly decant the jam mixture into scalded glass jars and add one boiled canning jar lid to each jar. Wait patiently for the "pop" of the can lid to tell you it has sealed. This is making jam. We made jam two batches at a time for three hours. We made twelve quarts and a few stray pints of jam for the girlchild and her partner, and untold pints for ourselves. Jar lids were pinging from the dining room all night.

We then all gathered around the table for a serving of hot biscuits under strawberries and whipped cream. We discussed the issues of the day: Can fresh strawberry jam be eaten with non-crunchy peanut butter? Should jam be eaten on bread, English muffins, or a naked spoon? What exactly is the "foam" that has been skimmed off, and does it really taste "funny" or do we just expect it to? What does the butter do? What would happen to peace in the Middle East, the price of tea in China, and global warming if a meal were served without the proper display of napkins?

And now: about those continents of starving children . . .

star bright

You go on hold
waiting
last minute consent forms
operations in the dead of night
waking at two in the morning
in an alien waiting room
to greet a doctor in green
who needs sleep
"She's recovering nicely
        the prognosis
        of course
        remains the same . . ."
WHICH WILL EVENTUALLY CAUSE
Chemotherapy, maybe
Radiation
        ("She may have already had
        too much . . ."
        Yes. And you lied about what
        it was for.)

Six phone calls to make
for every new decision
Six other people
love her
Six different approaches
"Is there anything I can do?"
The prognosis
—of course—
remains the same.

Can you cure cancer?
Sitting on the edge of her bed
holding her hand
teasing her about her bandage
around her head
which holds her skull
which holds her flesh
which is all her flesh
which is growing
rude, impudent flesh
arrogant cells, fighting for life
as she fights for life
crowding out the host life
which is hers
WHICH WILL EVENTUALLY CAUSE
She is recovering nicely.
She plucks wistfully at strings
in the air no one else can see
tidying her space
searching for words
words wrapped in growing flesh
smothered

lost
amputated
by malignant, irreverent cells.

I am a writer because my mother
loved to talk
talked endlessly
skillfully
Playing with words
like a kitten weaving herself
in among balls of string.
The word she is searching for now
is my name.
"Do you know who I am?"
She is aggravated: a stupid question
to ask a woman whose head is wrapped
in gauze
she conceived me
she birthed me
changed diapers and hemlines
wrapped me in her image
we are one
snarling, turning on each other,
straining at the umbilical cord
that never breaks between
WHICH WILL EVENTUALLY CAUSE
mother and firstborn
HER DEATH
no way in hell, Jack: you go on hold
waiting
of course she knows me.
"What is my name, Mom?"
She fingers invisible strings

like a lover caressing hair
Tips her hand to one side, defeated
"What is my name, Mom?"
Strangled.
By cells that are her cells
life turned malignant
irrevocably changed
crushing the life that gives life.

I can cure cancer.

I will go in there with a spoon
and dish out those cells
one by one
like scooping fish eggs
from the belly of a bluegill.
I will cut them out
with a razor and tweezers
like my sister removed
her plantar's wart.
I will cure it.
Burn it out.
Tear it out.
Drown it.
Crush it.
Strangle it.
She is my mother:
I am not done with her
yet.
I will not give her up.
I will not grant her permission
for her leaving me.
I will not

will not
will not
give her up
to mindless
ill-bred
thoughtless
self-destructive
cells.

Sitting on the edge of her bed
holding her hand
teasing her about her "bonnet"
willing her life
offering mine
willing her strength
willing her words to come
ACKNOWLEDGE ME, DAMNIT
She looks at me, startled
HAVE YOU FORGOTTEN WHO I AM?
DO YOU KNOW ME?
DO YOU LOVE ME?
DO YOU NEED ME?
CAN I HOLD YOU HERE WITH ME?
Can I keep it, Momma?
Can I kill it?
She pulls her hand from mine
frowning that baffled, injured frown
unlacing her fingers from mine
searching through the gauze that surrounds
her mind for lost words
I KNOW; YOU DON'T; DON'T ASK ME
I NEVER LIED TO YOU
SOMEDAY WHEN THINGS ARE CLEARER

fat girls and lawn chairs

I WILL CONFESS THE THINGS
I HAVEN'T SAID
She looks at me, betrayed
scolding
she says,
"Hurt."

Astrocytoma: wish upon a star.
Glittering lights in night skies
that see me home
the crests of Christmas trees
the guiding light
"You could have told us the first time."
"We don't like to tell a patient
they're terminal
          it has a tendency
to change their lives."
Astrocytoma: the star that kills.
The damage is done.
From here we wait
while twinkle, twinkle
little star
sucks dead
the host.
"We'll make her as comfortable
as we can."
You go on hold.
DON'T ASK ME NOW—
I NEED TO TALK IT OVER
WITH MY MOTHER.
You wait.
Try not to crush her hand
wishing on stars.

star bright
231

IT HAS
A TENDENCY
TO CHANGE
THEIR LIVES.
it has . . .

I've saved the pieces for you, Momma.
Someday when we're older
we'll sit together, thinking back
and I'll share my crooked irony:
"We never told you you were dying, Mom,
because we didn't want
to change your life."

God knows, we didn't.

"Is there anything we can do?"

You can give her
give me
our God-given right
to change
our own damned lives.

mother's day

THIS YEAR ON New Year's Eve, as we are ushering out the old and in the new, my family will celebrate the anniversary of my mother's death. We won't gather to acknowledge this milestone. There will be no big dinner. Each of us—each quite alone—will at some point during the day remember that something happened that changed the sense and texture of New Year's Eve forever. She died. The most vibrant, powerful—and occasionally exasperating—force in our lives lost her fight against cancer at the age of forty-nine on December 31, 1976.

I was, therefore, somewhat surprised to find her backstage with me last night. It has been a while since we did anything together.

My mother loved to perform. She was driven to achieve something with her life, to break out of the ordinary into the extraordinary. She wanted—needed—to be The Best at something and she wanted—and needed—the recognition that comes from that kind of success. Everything I know and feel about her, including my relationship to her, is colored by the sheer power of that single driving force. She was happiest when she was performing. When she gathered with her friends, it was my mother who gravitated toward the center of the room where, a little bigger than life, she starred in the joke or the tall tale or the anecdote she was telling. For twenty-five years she was a square-dance caller. When an image of her flashes through my mind, as often as not she is wearing her triple-tiered square-dance dress and holding a microphone in her hand as she shows her dancers a new step or call.

I remember her sitting on the living room couch facing her sister as they told each other stories about their lives and things they had seen and done since they last talked. They were both storytellers. The graceful, dramatic telling of the tale was at least as important as the tale itself.

I remember her sitting on the living room floor, laughing until tears ran down her cheeks as she read about the "nitch snitching nutchs in hutchs" of Dr. Seuss. To this day when I pick up a children's book and read to a child, it is my mother's cadence and rhythm the child hears.

I was spoon-fed my mother's love of words and language right along with my baby food. I spoon-feed my niece oatmeal with the same nonstop, nonsensical flurry of words and images that my mother fed me, as if words are food and language is sustenance.

I have never liked performing. Or, more accurately, I have rarely performed. There are a variety of reasons, none particularly well thought-out. First and foremost, you cannot be the very best at something without beating out all the competition and my mother was an intensely competitive woman. As her firstborn I was somehow destined to be her successor. I don't remember ever not knowing, in however childlike my way, that my mother was involved in some intense, not necessarily rational competition with me. I didn't know how to stop it or even what caused it. I didn't know how to ease her mind, so I called the only truce I could devise—I almost never attempted to excel in a field where she had shown an interest. I don't believe I ever sat down and made up a conscious list of Ways to Get Mother Off My Back—it was just some intuitive thing I did. She loved—and needed—to be center stage, so I stepped back and let her.

It served my purposes as well. I never needed to learn how to deal with the butterflies and the nerves and the upset stomach and the terror of forgetting everything you were supposed to do just as the audience sets you in their sights, because I never did it. I played Jo March in a sixth-grade production of *Little Women*, reveled in the limelight, and never stepped out on the stage again. I was a theatrical has-been at twelve.

Recently I have been writing more—shorter pieces that can be read in five or six minutes—and I have acquired friends who not only enjoy my writing, but enjoy hearing me read. When I mention I have written more, they request I read it to them aloud. This evolved, gradually, into the notion that I might read some of my work for the Phoenix Community Talent Show. I volunteered. It seemed like a good idea in February, when I had months to prepare and when I concentrated most of my efforts on writing the piece I might read. A month or so later it occurred to me I had volunteered to stand up, alone, in front of a veritable crowd of people, and **perform**.

Panicked, I chased down every friend I could find, tied them to a chair, and forced them to listen to me read my piece. My friends were all suitably supportive, but I knew in my heart that addressing a large crowd could be significantly different from reading to two or three people at a time. The response could be more/or less/or hostile/or flatline.

It could (Goddess forbid) be difficult.

But I had given my word, so I sweated through the program (having discovered I was second to the last to perform), and finally it was my turn to go backstage and hatch butterflies.

As I stood behind the curtain I remembered a conversation I had had earlier with a friend. She had just received permanent

Michigan custody of her father's car and she had just driven it for the first time here in this state. Before his death her father lived in California and both before and after his death she had driven his car in California—but suddenly, this evening driving the car had been difficult. Her father became more dead. She was driving stolen property. I told her that there had been a time when I had believed that grieving for someone was a one-time, get-it-over-with event and that after my mother's death I had been surprised to discover that over the years the experience changes, but it never really ends. There will always be something to remind you that this significant person in your life is missing a significant event she or he should have shared.

As I stood there behind the curtain I thought, "Of all the time you've been gone, Mom, this is the one night you really should have been here. After all the anger and confusion you felt over the anger and confusion I wrote so bitterly about while you were alive, it might amuse you to realize the things I write about now are actually funny. After all the concern you expressed over the fact that I never seemed to have a sense of who I was or where I was going, it might reassure you to realize that now—however late this is in my life—I am learning to hear and express my own voice. This is something you should have seen."

I stepped out onto the stage, making some lame note of introduction and I felt the audience hesitate, catch the humor of my remark and then laugh, and I remember thinking, "Well, we were right about that—this is NOTHING like reading to my friend Annie over her kitchen table."

And I stepped back and let my mother read.

about the author

CHERYL PECK lives with her cat, Babycakes, in Three Rivers, Michigan, where she does not grow tomatoes and rarely sits in lawn chairs. This is her first book. Cheryl originally self-published the book for her family and friends through a friend's vermicomposting and publishing company. This way if the book didn't sell, she could always use it for worm bedding.

KISS MY TIARA

How to Rule the World as a SmartMouth Goddess
by Susan Jane Gilman

A Cynthia Heimel for a new generation, Susan Jane Gilman serves up uncommon wisdom and practical advice on everything from sex to politics, from turning shopping skills into a power tool to using man-catching techniques for salary negotiations. Here are the smart rules for smart women of all cultures, sexualities, and sizes. Irreverent, provocative, hip—and always funny—this guide to power and attitude offers women an intelligient alternative to the negative messages we hear every day from magazines, television, and relatives.

"Don't you just love it when there's a wickedly smart BRAIN behind a wickedly smart MOUTH? *Kiss My Tiara* is dee-licious."

—Jill Conner Browne,
The Sweet Potato Queen's Book of Love